W9-CKI-612

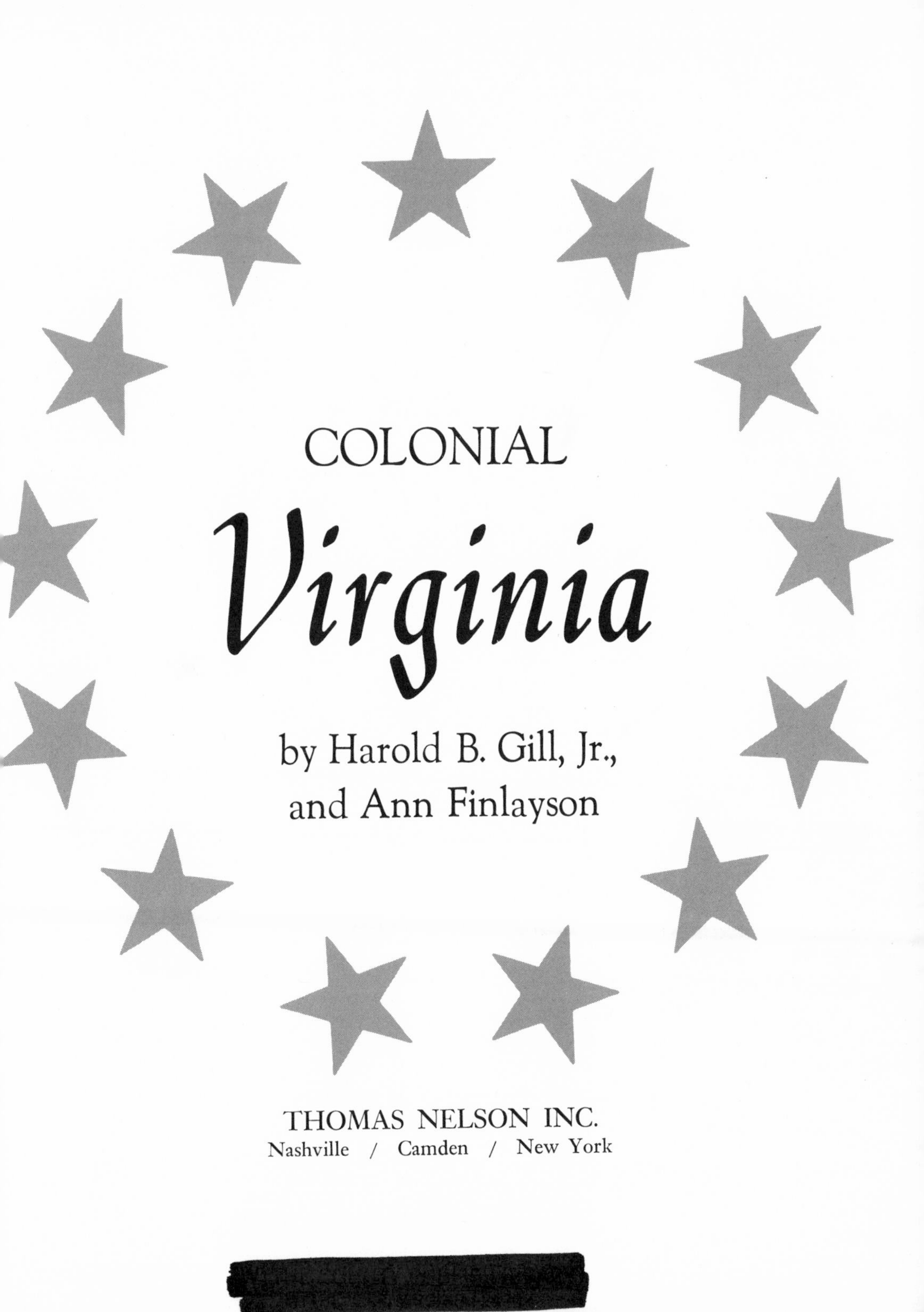

COLONIAL *Virginia*

by Harold B. Gill, Jr.,
and Ann Finlayson

THOMAS NELSON INC.
Nashville / Camden / New York

Photographs are from Colonial Williamsburg, with the exception of the following: pp. 8, 14, 24, 37, 45, 46, 49, 57, 60, 65, 98, 109, 134, 154 from the Virginia State Library; pp. 7, 11, 16, 17, 22, 31, 32–33, 102, 110, 113, 115, 118, 125, 137, 156 from the New York Public Library; pp. 76, 84, 88, 106 from Byrant & Gay, *Popular History of the United States* (photos by Virgil E. Row). Permission is gratefully acknowledged.

Published in Nashville, Tennessee, by Thomas Nelson Inc. and simultaneously in Toronto, Canada, by Thomas Nelson & Sons (Canada) Limited. Printed in the United States of America.

Second Printing

Library of Congress Cataloging in Publication Data

Gill, Harold B
Colonial Virginia.

(Colonial histories)
SUMMARY: Traces the history of Virginia from the landing of the first settlers in 1607 to Cornwallis' surrender at Yorktown in 1781.
Bibliography: p.
1. Virginia–History–Colonial period–Juvenile literature. [1. Virginia–History–Colonial period] I. Finlayson, Ann, joint author. II. Title.
F229.G5 975.5′02 72–13102
ISBN 0–8407–7114–2
ISBN 0–8407–7115–0 (NLB)

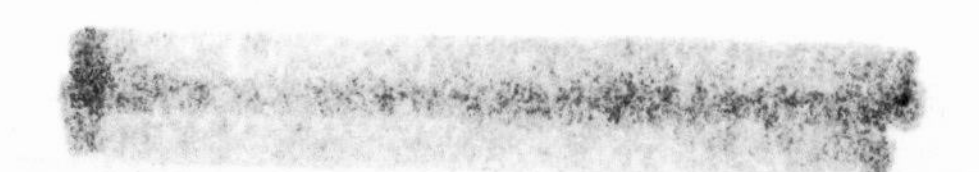

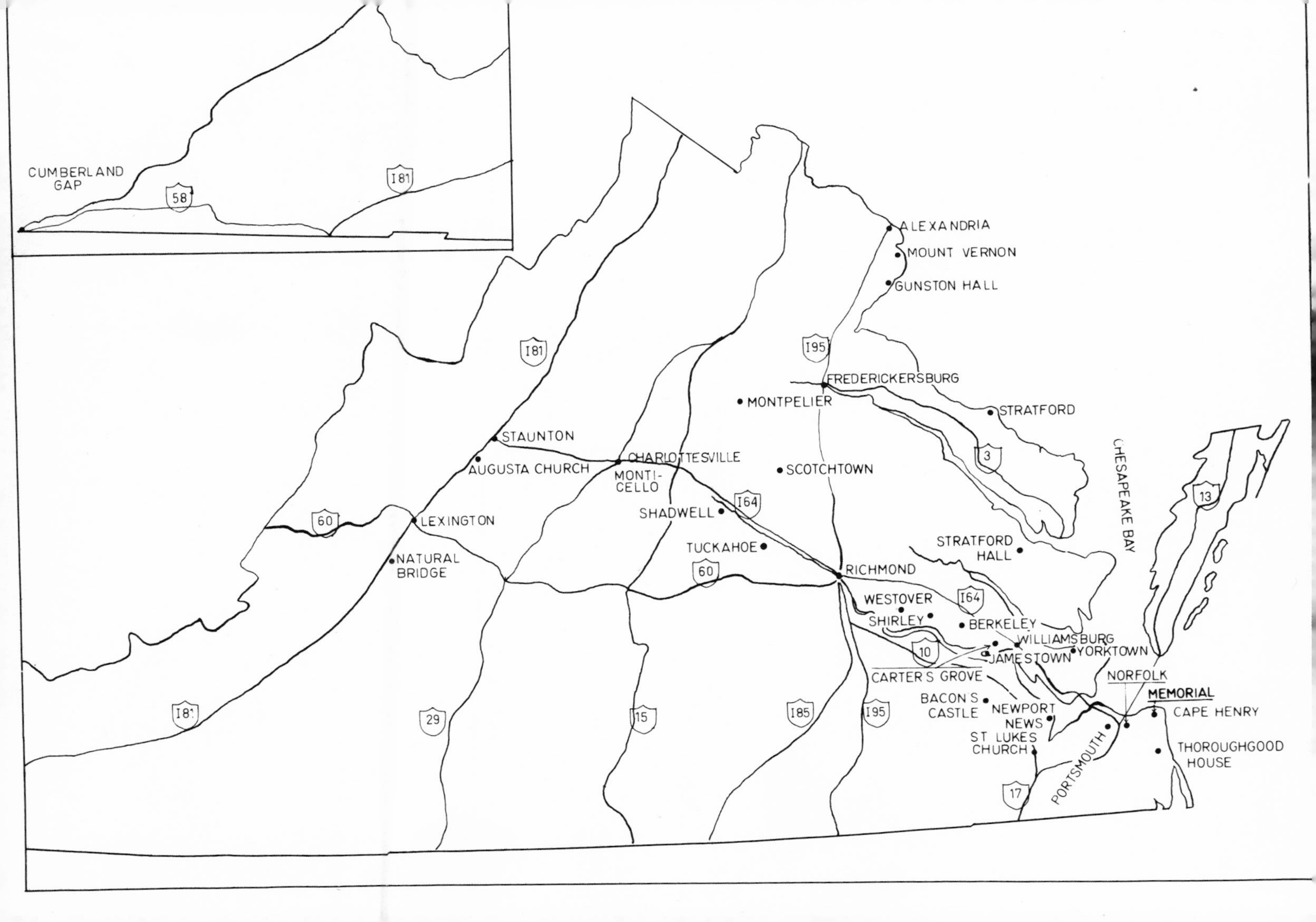

CUMBERLAND GAP
58
I81
ALEXANDRIA
MOUNT VERNON
GUNSTON HALL
I95
FREDERICKERSBURG
MONTPELIER
STRATFORD
STAUNTON
CHARLOTTESVILLE
AUGUSTA CHURCH
MONTI-CELLO
SCOTCHTOWN
3
CHESAPEAKE BAY
13
SHADWELL
I64
60
LEXINGTON
TUCKAHOE
NATURAL BRIDGE
STRATFORD HALL
RICHMOND
WESTOVER
SHIRLEY
BERKELEY
WILLIAMSBURG
10
JAMESTOWN
YORKTOWN
CARTER'S GROVE
NORFOLK
MEMORIAL
CAPE HENRY
BACON'S CASTLE
NEWPORT NEWS
ST LUKES CHURCH
PORTSMOUTH
THOROUGHGOOD HOUSE
29
15
I85
17

"The good Old Dominion, the mother of us all."

—Thomas Jefferson

Contents

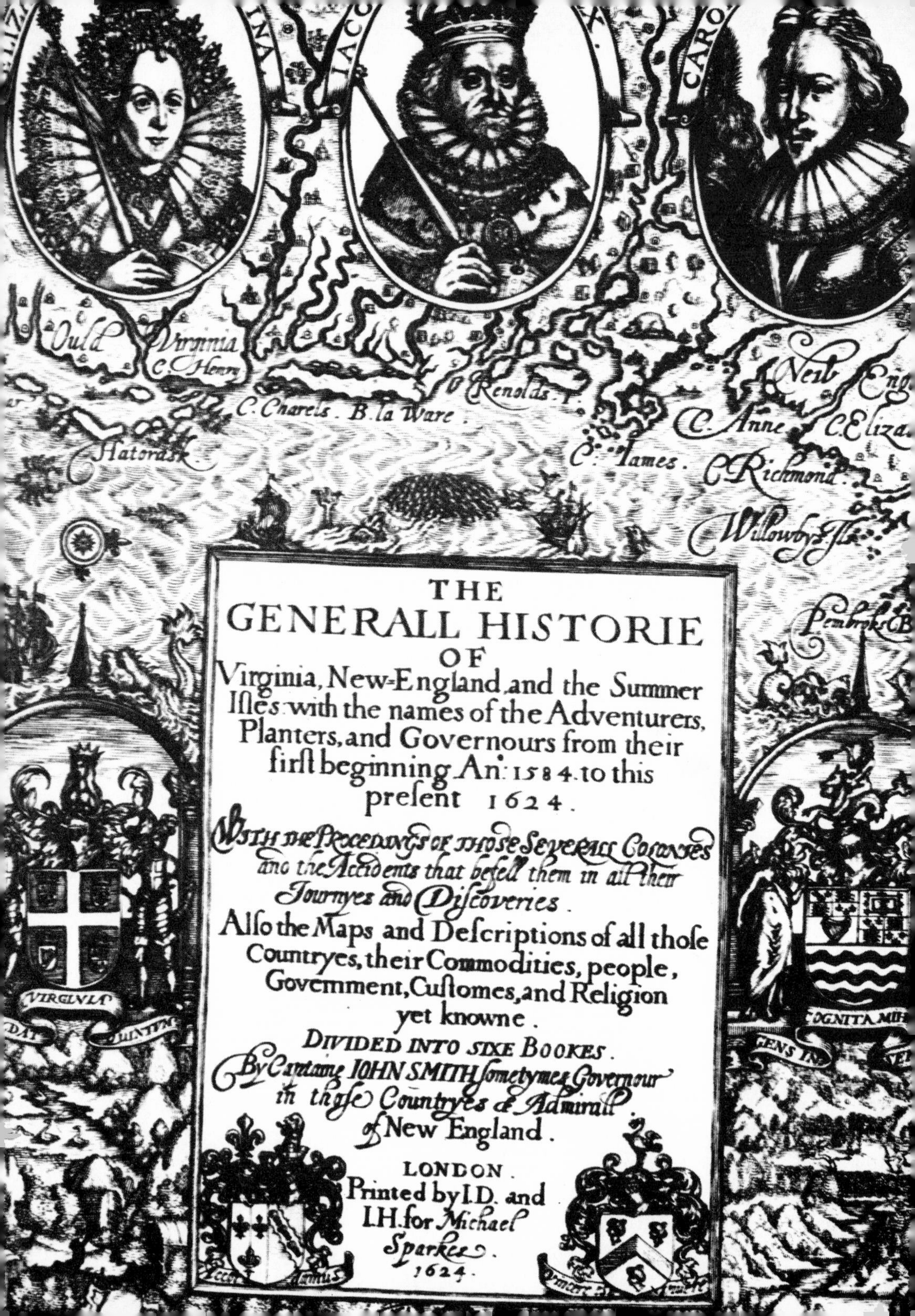

THE
GENERALL HISTORIE
OF
Virginia, New-England, and the Summer Isles: with the names of the Adventurers, Planters, and Governours from their first beginning An: 1584. to this present 1624.

With the Procedings of those Severall Colonies and the Accidents that befell them in all their Journyes and Discoveries.

Also the Maps and Descriptions of all those Countryes, their Commodities, people, Government, Customes, and Religion yet knowne.

DIVIDED INTO SIXE BOOKES.

By Captaine JOHN SMITH *sometymes Governour in those Countryes & Admirall of* New England.

LONDON.
Printed by I.D. and I.H. for *Michael Sparkes.*
1624.

CHAPTER ONE

A Perfict Peninsulla

On May 13, 1607, three small merchant ships edged close to a strange shore and anchored in six fathoms of water. Their "flagship," the *Susan Constant*, was a bare hundred tons burden, and her consorts, the *Godspeed* and the *Discovery*, a mere forty and twenty tons, respectively—even for their era, tiny vessels indeed.

There were no wharves available—nothing except forest and the broad expanse of tidal river—so the three made fast by tying up to trees along the bank. That done, their leaders held a council meeting to decide what to do next.

This strange shore was Virginia, in the New World, named in honor of the Virgin Queen, Elizabeth I, now dead. The purpose of this particular party was to make a settlement here. It would be the only English-speaking enclave along the coastline of thirteen thousand miles.

They did not know it was that long, of course, or even exactly where it ran. They only knew that in the hot regions to the south, the Spanish and Portuguese held dominion over thousands of gold-yielding acres and slave-laboring natives, and that in the cold regions to the north, the Dutch and French were opening a trade in fish and furs that promised a nearly equal wealth. The English did not want to miss out on the riches and power they could acquire in the New World. As a

Title page to John Smith's *Generall Historie of Virginia*, one of the first books ever written about North America.

The *Susan Constant*, *Godspeed*, and *Discovery* reach Virginia, bringing the first permanent white settlement in North America.

result, this little group was here in this wilderness—105 of them, all men—to plant their sovereign's flag, to make their private fortunes, and, if possible—if possible, for it was every adventurer's dream—to find the fabled shortcut to the Orient.

They decided to name their future settlement Jamestown, in honor of their monarch, James I, and to name the river on which it was to be situated the James. The site they had selected for a town was not the most promising in the world—a flat, marshy cape projecting out into the estuary. But the choice was not entirely their own. The little group had been sponsored and sent out by a private business venture called the London Company, backed by royal charter, and the Company had given its representatives some firm instructions.

They were to establish themselves at least one hundred miles up a navigable river, where the settlement would be safe from assault by sea, and yet close to deep water, so that a sizable supply vessel could anchor alongshore. It was to be an easily defensible site and a healthy one—that is, well removed from marshland. Marshes were widely known to give off disease-bearing "effluvia." The settlers were also to make sure that there were no natives living between this place—one hundred miles inland!—and the sea.

The voyagers on the three small ships had done their best, but the site was nevertheless a compromise. Jamestown was defensible but far from healthy; indeed, it was the neighboring marshes that *made* it defensible. It was scarcely more than fifty miles from the sea, because the deepwater provision had to be taken into account, and of course the colonists hadn't a hope of keeping out the Indians.

But it had its good points. "A perfict Peninsulla," one member of the expedition described it, "or tract of Land, all most wholly incompast with Water." There were oaks and beeches like those at home, as well as wild strawberries covering the ground, thickets of raspberries and brambles, and sturgeon in the rivers. To intrigue these men from cold, damp England, where viniculture had often been tried and had often failed, grapevines grew in lavish profusion. ("Vineland the Good," an earlier visitor had named America.) Moreover, there was exotic life new to them entirely: the mitten-leaved sassafras (believed to be a potent remedy for many ills), the bandit-masked raccoon, hickories, fireflies, muskrats, hummingbirds, the lush, pendulant wisteria. . . .

Having looked the place over, the council decided to unload first, then divide into two parties, one to explore, the other to build living quarters. So, the following day, May 14, they set about it.

Previous Settlements

The London Company's expedition was by no means the first attempt by the English to establish themselves in the Americas. In 1587 Sir Walter Raleigh and a group of noblemen and rich merchants received a grant of land from the Crown for a proprietary colony. Sir Walter and his colleagues were to transport the colonists to the New World and supply them until they had developed into a thriving community. But the first colony failed. Twice more Raleigh established colonies on Roanoke Island (in modern North Carolina), and each time they, too, failed. So did a similar English attempt to colonize what is now French Guiana.

But the Jamestown venture was to be different.

The First Council

Originally two companies had been chartered to form colonies in "Virginia"—as the bulk of southern North America was called—but only the London Company was actually able to launch an expedition. In addition to its instructions as to choice of settlement, the Company had named a council to rule the settlers. The list of councillors was kept sealed in a casket and throughout a long and unpleasant voyage had remained unknown. Now it was opened and found to name seven men: Christopher Newport, master of the *Susan Constant*, a one-armed seaman with long experience in American waters; Edward Maria Wingfield, the only member of the London Company to become an actual settler; Bartholomew Gosnold, master of the *Godspeed;* John Ratcliffe; John Martin, who had once sailed with Drake; George Kendall; and one Captain John Smith.

This last name came as an unpleasant surprise to the rest, who were either sea captains or had pretensions to being gentlemen. Indeed, on the voyage out, Wingfield had quarreled with Smith and had kept him imprisoned aboard ship. Now, of course, he had to be released, and almost immediately he began to make difficulties.

The Lincolnshire Soldier

John Smith was twenty-seven then—a short, stocky, blue-eyed individual with a fan-shaped beard, a mind of his own, and the annoying habit of knowing what he was talking about. Fate had plainly intended

Captain John Smith, soldier, adventurer, and savior of Jamestown.

the man for obscurity. For one thing, it had named him John Smith. For another, it had caused him to be the eldest son and heir of a prosperous farmer in Lincolnshire. When the father died in John's seventeenth year, the boy should have settled down on his comfortable inheritance, tilled his quiet acres, died and been buried, unknown, in the village churchyard. Instead, John Smith opted for adventure.

He traveled awhile on the Continent in the entourage of his father's patron. Then, because the one way in those days to make one's name—and one's fortune—was to do some fighting, he joined the only war he could find. The Ottoman Turks, who already held most of the Balkans, were trying to push their boundaries north and west to include the whole of Europe. They had crossed the Danube but were held at bay for a while in the Carpathian mountains by Hungary and other Christian nations. Smith enlisted with the Hungarians under Prince

Zsigmond Bathory and eventually was made a captain, which then meant a military leader over an unspecified number of soldiers. But on November 18, 1602, the prince's forces were overwhelmed at the Rotenturm Pass (in modern Romania), and Smith, along with other Christian prisoners, was marched off to Constantinople as an iron-collared slave.

According to his own account—historians argue over how accurate it is—he killed his Turkish master, escaped to Christian Russia, thence to Poland, Germany, France, Spain, North Africa, and ultimately England in 1604. There he learned that the old queen was dead and that the new king was planning to charter a company to settle in the New World on a profit-and-loss basis. John Smith signed up. Probably because of his military experience, the Company named him to its council.

Exploring the Countryside

Now, three years later, he had a difference of opinion with his fellow councillors. The others were anxious to carry out the Company's orders: to explore the area and locate gold or furs or the Pacific Ocean or sassafras or pearls or any other treasures that might turn the colony into a worthwhile investment. Smith wanted the expedition to concentrate its first efforts on making Jamestown safe from attack.

Already the settlers had suffered some minor sniping. While they were still seeking a site for their settlement, one of their landing parties had been attacked by Indians and several men wounded with arrows. On another occasion a band of braves, armed with clubs and stone-studded "swords," had prevented them from landing at all. Even while they were unloading the ship, stray natives wandered in from time to time, and there were "incidents." But Smith was overruled.

On May 21, while the greater part of the settlers were lazily setting up tents, digging gardens, and piling up a few boughs as rudimentary fortifications, a select group boarded the expedition's shallop—the shallow-draft small boat carried by most explorers for probing unknown streams—and set off with an Indian guide up the newly named James River. Despite his disapproval, Smith went along.

At first it was a pleasant voyage. It turned out that the newcomers' hostile reception had been all a mistake—or so the Indians said. Another English ship had recently visited the Rappahannock, killed several braves, and abducted several others. (Ships' captains often kidnapped "specimens" in this fashion and carried them off to be exhibited in Europe.) But now the Indians knew that *these* Englishmen were friends. To prove their friendship, they feasted them on deer meat and Indian corn and entertained them with dances. In return the English gave presents of hawks' bells, cheap knives, glass beads. They were intrigued by the life of these Virginia natives. Wrote one settler:

> They live comonly by the water side in little cottages of canes and reedes, covered with the barke of trees. . . . They live upon sodd wheat beanes & peaze for the most part, also they kill deare take fish in their weares [weirs; enclosures in the river for trapping fish], & kill fowle abundance, they eat often and that liberally; they are proper lusty streight men very strong runn exceeding swiftly. . . .

These villages were surrounded, the English visitors noted, with neat gardens of peas, beans, squash, Indian corn, and a tall, fragrant-flowered herb known to them by its Caribbean name: tobacco. Indians plucked the leaves of this plant, dried them, mixed them with other dried herbs, stuffed the mixture into reed pipes, and set fire to them, then inhaled the smoke. There was some religious significance to the action, but many seemed to derive pleasure from smoking. Some Englishmen tried the local product but found it harsh and rasping.

And so this pleasant intercourse went on for six days. Then their formerly friendly guide suddenly announced that he could go no farther. The English looked at one another. Newport, in command of the expedition, gave the order for a hasty return to Jamestown.

They arrived on May 27, to find that the settlement had been assaulted the day before. Indians from several villages had gathered near

A village of Virginia's native inhabitants, showing various aspects of Indian life.

the new town of tents and huts and had waited in ambush. Many of the settlers were working or loafing outside the flimsy barrier they had grumblingly erected. Suddenly the Indians pounced.

Before this, however hostile the Indians had been, their fear of the white man's matchlocks had made them hold back or withdraw speedily from an encounter. This time, discovering that guns took much longer to load than did bows and arrows, they pressed the attack with vigor. The whites fled. A boy fell dead and a man was fatally wounded; ten others were injured, and the jerry-built shelters were riddled with arrows. But just in time, the ships' guns opened up.

Terrified of the noise and the devastating grapeshot of the big guns, the Indians disappeared back into the woods. Jamestown survived—shakily. But the message was plain: John Smith had been right all along.

The Powhatan Confederation

With the military man to keep them at it, the new settlers got to work on a proper palisade, and by June 15 the fort was ready, triangular in shape and with three "Bulwarkes" at the corners. "Like a halfe Moone," one writer described these bastions, "and four or five pieces of Artillerie mounted in them. We made our selves sufficiently strong for these Savages."

He was right, for it was chiefly the Indians' respect for the strength of the fort and the power of the "Artillerie" that kept them from wiping out the newcomers that first summer. For these particular Indians, members of the close-knit Powhatan confederation, were formidable foes.

Most Virginia Indians belonged to the enormous Algonkian nation, the largest by many times of all the North American Indian language groups. The majority of Algonkian peoples lived scattered about the woodlands in small tribes, supporting themselves precariously by hunting, growing a few crops, making maple sugar in the spring. They weren't truly nomadic like the Plains Indians of a later era, but they moved their villages three or four times a year. They engaged in an animistic religion, went on the warpath nearly every summer, and were guided—not ruled—by chosen councils of elders and peace chiefs. They quarreled as often among themselves as with whites.

But the Powhatans, perhaps influenced by their sophisticated Muskogean neighbors to the south, had formed a league of closely allied tribes living in permanent villages along the York River, its tributaries, and the tributaries of the James. They were ruled by a single senior chieftain called the Powhatan. The leadership of this federation seems to have been hereditary, and the Powhatans apparently had the power to appoint werowances, or subchiefs, to head up the member villages. Unlike most Algonkian tribes, the Powhatans could summon large numbers of warriors at a given moment and could thus coordinate a powerful attack on the whites.

For the moment, however, they bided their time, hoping the invaders would get tired of Virginia and go away of their own accord. The English nearly did just that. Once the fort was completed, the settlers

Captain John Smith trades with the Indians for food to keep the starving colonists alive.

abandoned most of their labors. Gardens languished—many Jamestonians were gentlemen, and a gentleman did not hoe! A few tried to hunt, but they were poor at it, and their matchlocks were nowhere near so accurate as the Indians' bows. They did not even fish very efficiently or very often. They preferred to sit and bicker over who was in command, complain of the hot, damp climate, and wait until the supply ships returned.

Newport had sailed on June 22 with a cargo of what he thought might be gold. Fortunately he also took along some timber, for the "gold" turned out to be mica-flecked dirt, and it was the sale of the humble lumber that paid for the *Susan Constant*'s voyage. He did not get back to the anxiously waiting colony until the following January.

Meanwhile, the watching Indians kept track of what was going on. They came from time to time with gifts of meat—out of contempt or compassion or the desire to spy—and for a while they willingly traded their surpluses of corn and beans for the Englishmen's trinkets. When the little colony was swept by devastating illness—it is uncertain exactly what the disease was—they noted that, too. By September 10, nearly half the colony was dead, including Councillor Gosnold.

The little settlement was in bad shape. No houses had been built and winter would soon be upon them. Even with numbers reduced, they were starving. It was time for a strong man to take charge, and John Smith did not hesitate.

He "set some to mow," he wrote, "others to binde thatch; some to build houses, others to thatch them . . . so that, in short time, he provided most of them lodgings. . . ." That done, he set off by boat to trade for corn.

Smith's Great Adventure

Smith was a tough, shrewd little man. When he found that the Indians, aware that Jamestown was in desperate plight, offered only handfuls of corn for trade goods, Smith courageously said No. The Indians conferred, reconsidered the matter—and changed their tactics. When the

John Smith, about to be sacrificed, is saved by the intervention of thirteen-year-old Pocahontas. From Smith's *Generall Historie of Virginia.*

shallop pushed off, it was well laden with corn, oysters, fish, and venison.

This voyage was followed by others, also successful. Even the men who hated Smith most had to admit that it was chiefly he who kept them fed. He did particularly well among the Indians living along the Chickahominy River. These tribes did not belong to the Powhatan federation and welcomed the white men. Trading cagily, taking care not to appear too eager, Smith brought back boatload after boatload of corn. Finally one day in December, 1607, he went too far and ran into Powhatan territory again. His companions were killed, and he was carried off a prisoner.

His captor was Opechancanough, half brother to the Powhatan, and in his way just as tough, shrewd, and implacable as John Smith. He might have killed the captain then and there. Instead, after testing out his courage and running him about from place to place, he took the prisoner to the Powhatan himself. What followed was one of the most romantic episodes in the history of the New World.

The scene was a large lodge, where the chief men sat along the side walls, and the great chief, covered with a robe of raccoon skins, sat enthroned on a pile of mats. Women were present too, standing behind their men and decked in finery of paint and pearls. Near the chief sat his favorite daughter, a youngster of twelve or thirteen. Her name was Matoaka, but her disposition was so lighthearted and lively that she was better known by her nickname, Frolicsome—in her native tongue, Pocahontas.

There was some shouting and ceremonial feasting, then Powhatan questioned the Englishman. Why were the strangers here? What did they want? How long would they stay? Smith lied stoutly: They had been driven ashore by a storm. They would go away—soon. Whether Powhatan believed him or not is unknown, but Smith reported what happened next in his own words:

> Two great stones were brought before Powhatan; then as many as could layd hands on him [Smith], dragged him to them and

> thereon laid his head . . . [The braves] being ready with their clubs to beate out his braines, Pocahontas, the King's dearest daughter . . . got his head in her arms, and laid her owne upon his to save him from death: whereat the Emperor was contented he should live. . . .

Historians have called Smith a liar for this story, but modern ethnologists think it more likely that the scene actually took place but that Smith misunderstood it, that what he underwent was a kind of ritual adoption. Indians of all nations frequently adopted outsiders, especially those they regarded as superior to the general run in strength, courage, and cunning. In any event, they let Smith go free.

Hard Times

The night after Smith arrived back at Jamestown, Captain Newport returned from London with provisions and what is called the First Supply of settlers. Only 38 of the original 105 were still alive. Five days

Map of Virginia as it appears in John Smith's *A True Relation*, published in England in 1608.

later the unlucky little colony suffered one more calamity: At the coldest season of the year, a fire "consumed all the buildings of the fort, and the storehouse of ammunition and provision." Only three of Smith's laboriously built dwelling houses remained standing.

But they were at least at peace with the Indians. The natives brought food, and Powhatan even sent some of his men to teach the settlers how to plant corn and make fish traps. Somehow they held on through their first winter.

In April, Newport set sail again for England, laden with more of what the colonists hoped would turn out to be gold. (It didn't.) Another ship, the *Phoenix*, stopped by in June and departed carrying a cargo of cedar and a manuscript that Captain John Smith, in between all his other duties, had contrived to write: *A True Relation of Such Occurrences and Accidents of Noate* [Note] *as Hath Hapned in Virginia since the First Planting of That Collony*, published that same year as the first printed account of the new settlement.

That summer, the same devastating sickness swept through the colony. In October, 1608, Newport returned with the Second Supply of settlers, more provisions, and instructions to get busy and find the route to the Pacific Ocean. There were also hints that the Company was getting tired of investing all this money and effort in an enterprise that had brought them no profit. Where was the gold? Where were the fur and fish? Taking the small boats, Newport went exploring, leaving houses unbuilt, settlers bewildered and quarrelsome.

The First Supply had contained 33 out of 120 members who listed themselves as "gentlemen." In the Second Supply, there were 28 out of 70. Such men were useless to the colony, John Smith felt. He wrote:

"When you send again, I entreat you rather send but thirty Carpenters, husbandmen, gardiners, fishermen, blacksmiths, masons and diggers up of trees, roots, well provided, than a thousand of such as we have."

But as fast as men landed, they died off, sometimes by drowning or accidents, or being cut down by the Indians in isolated parties, but mostly by the dread summer sickness.

Food was still scarce, but Smith, now tacitly acknowledged leader of the little group, managed to get a well dug inside the fort and a blockhouse built. With the arrival of spring, he saw to it that a good crop of corn was planted. And in August, 1609, seven ships arrived at Jamestown, bringing four hundred passengers—among them the first women—and more supplies. A new order was about to be established.

The Gates Expedition

The Company in England had recognized that the useless, unruly, unhealthy colony needed a firm hand. It had obtained from the king a new charter abolishing the local council and arranging for the appointment of a single governing head. The first such "Lord Governor and Captain General of Virginia" was to be Thomas West, third Baron de la Warr (or Delaware).

As an immediate, emergency measure, Delaware ordered out a fleet of nine ships under the command of Sir Thomas Gates. Only seven arrived—the seven mentioned above—for the rescue mission ran into a hurricane and one ship foundered and another, carrying Gates himself, was cast ashore on Bermuda. Gates and his fellow survivors spent the following winter building two small vessels and continued their voyage to Virginia in the spring, arriving on May 20, 1610.

(When news of their adventures in "the vexed Bermoothes" reached London, it inspired the popular dramatist William Shakespeare to write one of his last plays, which he called *The Tempest.*)

Gates found calamity facing him in Virginia. Of the four hundred sent by Lord Delaware, in addition to all settlers still living from previous "Supplies," only sixty-five men survived. John Smith, injured in a powder explosion, had returned to England the autumn before, and without him the colony had gone to pieces. "The starving time," the winter of 1610 was always called thereafter. Gates found the palisades gateless and in ruins, half the houses empty, the chapel fallen into decay. Sickness, lack of food, increasingly bold attacks by the Indians—it was all too much for the leaderless and desperate settlers. They wanted to return to England.

Gates tried for two weeks to persuade the disheartened colonists to stick it out a little longer. But corn was scarce that spring, even among the Indians, and soon the sickly season would be upon them. No, they would not be convinced. On June 10, 1610, they abandoned their broken-down stockade with its "Bulwarkes," put their meager belongings aboard ship, and sailed down the James for home.

But they never got there. On the way downriver, they encountered Lord Delaware himself, just arrived from England with a fleet of three ships, fresh supplies, and 150 more settlers. The new lord governor took immediate command of the colony and sternly ordered the Jamestonians back to their settlement. The English standard was not to be driven from American shores so easily as *that!*

New Policies

Back at Jamestown, the governor rebuked the settlers for vanity and idleness and pledged himself to invoke stern measures, if necessary, to force them to work and save themselves. Under his driving force, the fort was strengthened, the chapel was restored, sturdier houses were built.

These "houses" were nothing like the solid, comfortable log cabin of later days, introduced by Swedish settlers on the lower Delaware River

Wattle-and-daub church reconstructed at Jamestown, in the style of the original dwellings.

in 1643. Instead, Jamestown settlers built half-timbered structures such as English peasants lived in.

A solid frame of crude wood, hacked out with an ax, was erected and cross-braced for additional strength. Then the space between the frames and braces was filled in with wattle and daub. Wattle was a kind of woven wood, with upright sticks to form the "warp" and flexible twigs intertwined between them to form the "weft." Daub was a clay-and-straw mixture plastered over this primitive lath. A thatched roof of straw and a "country chimney" of logs lined with clay completed the building.

Such houses were often very small—some barely six feet high and twelve feet wide. Thin-walled, flimsy, easy to set afire; to the early colonist, an exile far from home in a dangerous and sickly land, they must have offered little coziness and less protection.

But the colony survived. And when Lord Delaware left for England in March, 1611, and Sir Thomas Dale, a veteran soldier, arrived as deputy governor, it began to gain in strength.

Henrico and Bermuda Hundred

Dale was a disciplinarian. He had heard enough tales of lazy and unproductive colonists, and when he arrived in May to find that Jamestonians had reverted to their old selves within two months—the corn unplanted, the men "at their usuall and daily works, bowling in the streets"—he put the colony under a strict code. "Dale's Laws" provided severe penalties for any settler who shirked his duties. Moreover, Sir Thomas introduced a new land policy.

Before this, all land at Jamestown had been held and worked in common, and each settler had received his rations from a common store. Dale saw that this system discouraged enterprise, rewarding the lazy man equally with the one who worked hard. Sir Thomas began to grant the more industrious settlers small private garden plots where they could grow extra crops for their own use.

Almost immediately the food supply began to increase. The little colony spread beyond its triangular stockade, and the palisade had to be enlarged to include the new houses and their gardens. As the colony increased in strength, Dale set about finding sites for new settlements, less unhealthy than marshy Jamestown. For Dale was in agreement with Captain John Smith: The settlers had to make themselves safe before they started making themselves rich.

He found one site at a hairpin bend of the James, where the river, twisting and turning, formed a series of narrow peninsulas. He selected one of these peninsulas, which he named Henrico, after Henry, Prince of Wales, and established settlers there. They ditched the narrow neck and built blockhouses along the river's edge and soon had the area so strongly fortified that it was all but immune to Indian attack. From there, Dale had them run a protective line of forts across to the falls of the Appomattox River, a distance of ten miles, isolating another, even

Nicotiana tabacum—tobacco—this humble plant provided all the wealth, and more, that settlers had hoped to derive from gold.

larger peninsula from easy assault. They called this area Bermuda Hundred, after Gates's castaway island, "hundred" being an old English term for a jurisdictional district.

Henrico and Bermuda Hundred gave the English settlers many miles of safe, healthy land where they could grow food, build up population, and strengthen their feeble, by-the-fingertips grasp of a piece of the New World. They could even experiment with new crops.

Road to Riches

One such experimenter was a man who had come over with Gates—Master John Rolfe, son of a Norfolkshire squire. He settled in Virginia and in 1611 obtained some seeds from Trinidad, with a view to trying them out in North American soil. The seeds were those of a kind of tobacco native to Central and South America: *Nicotiana tabacum*, first cousin to the *Nicotiana rustica* raised by the Powhatans and other local Indians but—as advertisers' claims were to put it many years later—"milder, much milder."

Rolfe planted the new species, raised the plants, tried out various methods of curing the leaf, and in 1613 sent part of his crop to England. It was tested by experts—importers of Spanish and Portuguese tobacco—and pronounced excellent. For the first time, a cargo of products from Virginia sold for a solid profit.

When the news reached Jamestown, settlers abandoned the search for gold, for fish and fur, for a shortcut to the Orient. They planted tobacco instead. The Company had found its road to riches.

CHAPTER TWO

The Taking-in of the Smoke

Tobacco and the Indians' habit of smoking had been known in Europe for over a hundred years before Jamestown was founded. Columbus was offered leaves of tobacco on his second day in the New World. Among some Indian cultures, Spanish explorers reported, the leaf was carefully grown and cured, treated with reverence, employed in religious ceremonies. Among others, use was much more casual; a man would tear a few leaves off a growing plant, twist them into a cone, and light the broad end, thus forming a primitive cigar. Often the leaf was chewed, usually along with coca leaves.

The habit of smoking—like many other dubious things, including numerous contagious diseases—was spread around the world by sailors. The Spanish smoked cigars, while Portuguese and English seamen preferred pipes. Toward the latter part of the sixteenth century, English gentlemen of fashion began to experiment with smoking—or "quaffing the fume," as it was called. "In these daies the taking-in of the smoke of the Indian herbe called Tobacco, by an instrument formed like a little ladell . . . is gretlie taken up and used in England," wrote a chronicler in 1573. Many ladies of Elizabeth's court smoked pipes.

The Spanish prepared their leaf in a number of elaborate ways—formed it into balls or pigtail twists or thick rolls, soaked it in rum, molasses, sugar, or wine, and sometimes blended it with the leaves of other plants. In England, it became the fashion to boast of the grade of "Spanish" that one "quaffed." And, indeed, a man had to be rich to buy the imported leaf. In 1599 the best grades sold for £4 10*s* per pound, the equivalent of many weeks' wages for a workingman.

Apothecaries flourished in colonial days. Among their many herbal remedies, tobacco played an important part.

But except among gallants and sailors, tobacco's first widespread use was as a medicine. It was an age when people believed that anything strongly scented or flavored had to be a remedy for *something*. Physicians and herbalists—men who specialized in the growing and using of herbs and wrote treatises about it—advocated smoking to relieve asthma, bronchitis, dropsy, headaches, constipation, epilepsy, "ailments of the breast." Some thought it strengthened the memory. Ointments made of tobacco were applied lavishly to skin ulcers and ringworm. Sickly young Francis II, King of France and first husband of Mary Queen of Scots, is believed to have died of nicotine poisoning, from a tobacco ointment applied to heal him of some other complaint.

Tobacco had its enemies, of course. The patriarch of the Russian Orthodox Church pronounced smoking a mortal sin, and the czar obligingly sent persistent offenders to Siberia. In India—for the Portuguese had carried tobacco to the Far East before 1600—the Mogul Emperor Jahangir ordered that smokers should have their lips slit. Anyone caught importing leaf into China was beheaded. In 1605 a public debate was held at Oxford, England, among learned men of the day, in which the antitobacco forces presented the blackened organs of deceased smokers as evidence for their case. The previous year, King James himself had published a famous denunciation of the smoking habit, *Counterblaste to Tobacco*, in which he called smoking ". . . a custome lothsome to the eye, hatefull to the nose, harmefull to the braine, daungerous to the lunges, and in the blacke, stinking fume thereof, neerest resembling the horrible Stigian smoke of the pit that is bottomless."

But people continued to smoke. So the king did the next best thing to abolishing the habit—he taxed it heavily. The duty on imported "Spanish" was raised from 2*d* per pound to 6*s* 10*d*. Naturally, Englishmen preferred to smuggle tobacco rather than pay such horrendous rates. Then, just as the smuggling business was getting well launched, John Rolfe's first shipment of "Virginia" arrived in London.

Thereafter, the fortunes of both colony and crop were to rise and fall together.

Staple Crop

Tobacco growing, as it was understood in the seventeenth century, was not a difficult art. "Tabaco must be sown in the most fruitfull ground that may be found," wrote John Gerard, an early herbalist, "carelessly cast abroad in sowing, without raking it into the ground, or any such pain or industry taken as is requisite in the sowing of other seed." While the seedlings were small, they had to be kept free of weeds, but thereafter, being tall, big-leaved plants, they took their share of sun and rain naturally and needed comparatively little cultivation. Before the plant flowered, the flower bud was picked off, a practice called topping, which caused the plant to cease growing taller and firmed up the leaves already opened. Two months or so after topping, the leaf was ready to harvest and cure.

The plant was cut green. At first, novice planters simply gathered the leaves into heaps on the ground and let them dry in the sun, then rolled them up into loose bundles and shipped them. But this system caused the leaf to rot or crumble into mold long before it reached London. After some experimentation, planters learned to dry the leaves on racks out of doors, then cure them in tobacco houses.

Within four years of Rolfe's first shipment, tobacco was being grown on every patch of ground that could be spared. For a while, even the streets of Jamestown were planted with tobacco. Wherever a few acres could be made secure—"in the Curles of the River," as one writer put it—nothing was grown but tobacco, tobacco, tobacco. Sir Thomas Dale had to order the heedless colonists to set aside some acreage on which to grow food, or they would have neglected corn crops entirely.

The London Company was a trifle dubious about this single-minded obsession with one crop, but its interest in Virginia revived, and it began to advertise enthusiastically for colonists. To encourage people to emigrate, the Company adopted and expanded Sir Thomas Dale's land policy. Every stockholder of the Company in England received a hundred acres of land for every share. Every settler with seven years' residence in Virginia received the same. Furthermore, the Company offered fifty acres to every individual who would travel to the colony at his own expense and another fifty acres for each additional person he brought over. Thus was established the headright system, which continued to be the colony's land policy throughout the century. It accomplished its goal: It peopled the infant colony with laboring men.

Soon the little immigrant ships were crossing the ocean with their human cargoes. Between 1619 and 1625, over four thousand Englishmen packed up and moved to Virginia.

It was not uncommon for men of some means to risk their money and goods on the chance of finding a greater estate in the New World. If a merchant or artisan could pay passage for himself, his wife, and his son, he could start out as a freeman with title to 150 acres—a large holding by the standards of land-hungry England. And he could easily buy more, for in Virginia land was cheap and labor expensive.

But far more immigrants arrived as indentured servants, brought over by planters already established. By this means, the "importer" not only obtained a bondman's services for a period of years—usually four—but could claim an extra fifty acres headright for each man. His serving time up, the former bond servant might continue to work for wages, but he was far more likely to set up for himself on the fifty acres to which he was entitled.

Peace and Prosperity

Land obviously could not be planted until it had been cleared. There were some natural meadows near the great Virginia rivers, but most of the new colony was primeval forest—thickly grown with full-sized hardwood trees, which had to be cut down and underbrush removed to make room for the little plantations that were beginning to appear along the waterways. This was backbreaking work, but once established, an industrious man could live rather well.

If he had been foresighted and rich enough to bring cattle and pigs with him, he found that these animals thrived. The pigs were marked and turned loose to forage in the woods and only rounded up at slaughtering time. For a good hunter, there were deer and wild turkeys, geese, duck, quail, pheasant. The rivers abounded with fish and the salt marshes with succulent terrapin. Corn and vegetables grew well in the virgin soil. As long as there was peace, only a lazy man starved.

There were some drawbacks. Sheep were not such successful imports as pigs, because sheep need a lot of open pastureland. And flax, although it grew wild in Virginia and was easily cultivated, required such enormous efforts to transform it into linen that it was not at first considered worth growing. So, for clothing and blankets, as well as tools, a new settler was dependent on the mother country. But to obtain these he had his cash crop, tobacco.

There was money to be made in tobacco in those early years. In 1617 the *George* carried twenty thousand pounds of it to England, where it sold for *5s 6d* a pound and made a fortune for the Company and the planters.

At first only poor Englishmen bought "Virginia," while the rich snubbed the colonial product and insisted on "Spanish." But something about the soil and the climate of southern North America was exactly suited to the growing of tobacco, and once methods of planting and curing were improved, "Virginia" began to gain on her rival. (An early convert was the Indian, who abandoned his own native species, except for ceremonial occasions, in favor of the white man's leaf.) "Virginia" was much, much cheaper than "Spanish," of course, but it had another advantage over the imported leaf: an odor so pleasant that, when it came time to give the variety a distinguishing name—to set it apart from the Oronoco grown chiefly in Maryland—it was called Sweet Scented. It was this natural fragrance that won many smokers. Within a decade "Spanish" was a rarity in England.

Love Affair

Virginia could not have prospered so easily or so fast, of course, if she had been plagued with relentless Indian wars. Until 1613, in fact,

"The king's dearest daughter" —Pocahontas—poses in European dress during a visit to England with her English husband.

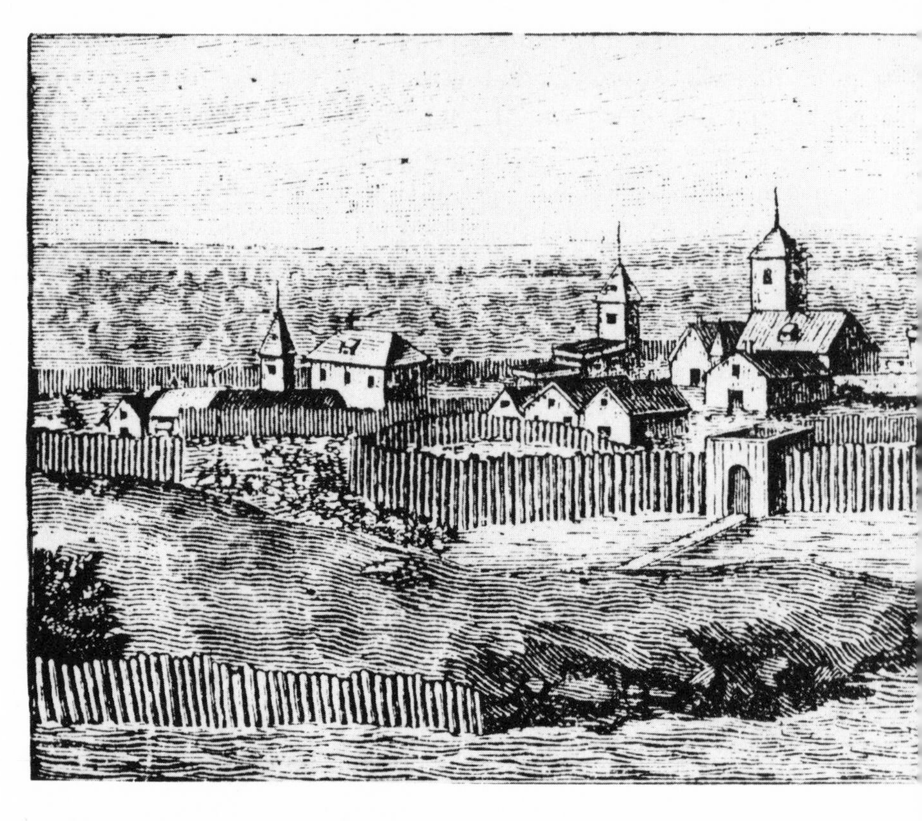

The little colony had already spread beyond its first triangular palisade when this sketch of Jamestown was made by a visiting Dutchman.

the colony did suffer a series of raids, and reckless settlers who left the protected areas to take up land were often killed or made prisoner. But in the spring of that year, a sea captain in the Company's service managed to kidnap and carry off to Jamestown an important Indian hostage —none other than young Pocahontas, then eighteen. Terrified for the safety of his daughter, Powhatan released some white captives and promised to keep the peace.

Pocahontas was well treated by Sir Thomas Dale, who was charmed by her, and she allowed herself to become converted to Christianity and

be baptized Rebecca. Some time that same year, she met Master John Rolfe, the tobacco developer, and he proposed a marriage of state between them. "For the good of the plantation," he said but admitted that he was very much in love: "My heartie and best thoughts are . . . so intangled and inthralled in so intricate a laborinth that I was awearied to unwinde myself."

The girl was willing, and when word was sent to her father, he agreed, too, and sent her uncle and two brothers to represent him at the wedding in April, 1614. Both sides seemed to regard this little romance as an omen of peace, and for eight years there was no warring. They were eight fortunate years for the colony.

Pocahontas herself did not live to see them end. Rolfe took his wife to England in 1616, where she was introduced at court in European dress. The king and many others in rank-conscious England were not altogether pleased with the marriage—after all, she was a princess and he was the merest commoner, barely a gentleman—but the couple were received graciously enough. Then, just after they had boarded ship to return to Virginia, Pocahontas fell ill. The disease was one that was just then beginning to ravage Europe in a series of devastating epidemics: smallpox. In a few days the bright little creature was dead. She left an only son, Thomas Rolfe, who was raised in England but in time returned to his mother's homeland to found a long line of distinguished Virginians.

Democracy and Slavery

The eight years of peace were important to Virginia, not only to allow tobacco to establish itself as a staple, but to bring far-reaching reforms in government. For in 1619 a new governor, Sir George Yeardley, arrived at Jamestown with instructions to set up a general assembly. It was to have two houses, an upper body consisting of the governor's council (already well established) and a lower body composed of representatives of the eleven "burroughs" or administrative districts into which the colony was to be divided. This House of Burgesses was to meet yearly at the capital to "make and ordaine whatsoever lawes and orders should by them be thought good and profittable." Since two representatives were allowed to each "burrough," the first House of Burgesses contained twenty-two members.

Its first meeting was held on July 30, 1619, in a Jamestown church, where it adopted measures to prohibit gambling, drunkenness, swearing, and idleness. It required every settler to attend church regularly and discouraged extravagance by imposing a tax on the value of the clothes a man and his wife wore to church. The burgesses were to legislate on Indian affairs, land patents, agriculture, the price of tobacco—anything relating to the general welfare of the colony. Such enactments were subject to veto by the governor or the London Company—later the king. But an important precedent had nonetheless been set.

Henceforth, Virginians were to have some hand in governing themselves.

Another precedent was set that same year, an ugly one but in its way just as far-reaching as the other: A Dutch man-of-war stopped off at Jamestown and sold the colonists twenty African Negroes. These first black immigrants were considered in the same category as white bondmen, and after a period of servitude they were set free—many ocean miles from home and kindred, of course—and it was to be a long time before slavery really took hold in Virginia. But, ominously, it had been found that blacks could be made to work more easily than Indians, who died under forced labor, and that they withstood the sickly season better than Europeans. So, democracy for whites and slavery for blacks had their first little beginnings at almost the same moment.

Diversification

Officials of the Company, still uneasy at the idea of a one-crop economy, had been urging its colonists to diversify. Moreover, the mother country hoped that Virginia would produce many of the goods that England was then importing from the Continent and the Far East. Timber, tar, and barrel staves for ship's stores were produced and sent home. Brick and pottery works were set up for local use, and as early as 1611, several houses in Jamestown employed brick in place of wattle and daub. But one by one the more exotic projects petered out.

Glassmaking was difficult in England, because wood needed to fuel the furnaces had grown scarce there. Virginia had plenty of wood, however, so the Company hired and sent over glassworkers from Poland to teach colonists the craft. When this first venture failed (for reasons unknown), they imported a new set of artisans from Italy. These Italians hated life in the primitive settlement, and they declared the Virginia sand unsuited to glassmaking and demanded to be sent home. To put the matter beyond argument, they deliberately smashed their furnace.

American wild grapes had too gamy a flavor to make good wine—

fox grapes, wine lovers called them with disdain—and the market for sassafras was limited. Animals native to the mild southern climate did not produce thick fur. An effort was made to establish silk-making in the colony, taking advantage of the fact that mulberries, on which the silkworm feeds, grew profusely in the New World. But labor was too scarce for so exacting an art, and eventually it was abandoned.

The most promising enterprise was the blast furnace erected upriver from Henrico, where iron ore had been found. Enthusiastically the Company sent over English workmen to mine and smelt the mineral into pig iron. But just as this project was getting under way, calamity fell on the unsuspecting colonists: the Indian massacre of 1622.

Massacre

Powhatan had died in 1618, and his place had been taken by his half-brother, Opechancanough, the captor of Captain John Smith eleven years earlier. This chieftain hated the whites with consuming bitterness. He had watched the immigrant ships sail up his native rivers to unload more and more of the newcomers, had seen them spread out beyond the palisades of Henrico and Bermuda Hundred to settle confidently wherever they chose, cut down the forest, kill the game, replace the Indians' bark shelters with their own strange houses. Perhaps he could foresee that it was now or never for the Indian, that if the English and their settlements were not exterminated immediately, while still relatively weak, they would soon overrun the land.

Whatever his reasoning, he planned his uprising with masterly care. The English were few and scattered, but they possessed those deadly guns. Surprise was the chief's only hope. Warriors were therefore summoned from all over eastern Virginia and secretly dispatched to the various English settlements. The whites were entirely unsuspicious, and to keep them that way, Opechancanough sent a message to Jamestown that peace was so firmly established between red man and white that the sky "should sooner fall than it dissolve." Right up to the last moment, he took pains to appear friendly to those whites he encoun-

The massacre of 1622. At more than eighty locations, the Indians fell on settlers and slew every living person.

tered personally. Then, on the morning of March 22, 1622, he gave the signal for his "deadly stroake."

Simultaneously at more than eighty separate locations, the Indians set upon the English and slew men, women, and children. They caught farmers preparing tobacco patches, workmen making brick, carpenters sawing, housewives at their chores, and killed them with clubs or arrows before they could get to their matchlocks. The ironworkers were wiped out to a man and their furnace thrown down. In some places the Indians came into English houses as though to trade or share breakfast, as they were accustomed to do, and then dispatched the family with their own tools. In their unleashed fury, the warriors sometimes hacked and chopped at the corpses of their victims long after death.

Out of the thousands of Indians who were in on the plot, only one gave away the secret. A Christian Indian boy named Chanco confessed to his master on the evening of March 21. The Englishman, by frantic rowing, got to Jamestown in time to warn the capital, so that the settlers there were able to defend themselves successfully. But more than three hundred others died, including John Rolfe and six of the governor's councillors.

It was the end of peace between red man and white. For the time being, it was the end of tobacco prosperity. And ultimately it was the end of the London Company.

CHAPTER THREE

Child of the Kingdom

The uprising sent the terrified settlers flying back to the protection of their fortifications, and the government ordered all occupied buildings and settlements to be surrounded with *pallyzados*—stout log walls set four feet into the ground and rising seven or eight feet above it. Crowded together in this fashion, the colonists could not plant crops or hunt, and soon famine was upon them again. Moreover, the crowding made them easy prey to the plague that arrived with new immigrant ships that same spring. Hunger and disease between them killed off many times as many people as had the Indians.

But after the first panic had subsided, the settlers began to retaliate on the Indians. The light-footed warriors could vanish quickly into the forests, but they could not move the growing corn on which they depended. The English under Governor Yeardley began to raid their villages, burning the "little cottages of canes and reedes" and destroying crops. A long-drawn-out struggle ensued, with savage reprisals on both sides.

The Virginia coastline is little more than a fringe of peninsulas formed by her four great rivers: Potomac, Rappahannock, York, and James. Because these rivers are tidal estuaries, fed by an intricate system of creeks and marshes, the whole coastal lowland region is called Tidewater Virginia. And in the seventeenth century, this geography was the colonists' best ally in their fight with the Indians. Ships could sail far inland, overawing the natives with their big guns. Even a light shallop could mount a fairly formidable cannon. Gradually the English drove the

VIRGINIA
MARYLANDIA
et
CAROLINA
IN AMERICA SEPTENTRIONALI
Britannorum industria excultæ
repræsentatæ
à
Ioh. Bapt. Homann S.C.M. Geog.
Norimbergæ
Septentrio
Occidens
Oriens
PENSYLVANIÆ
PARS
MARY LAND
VIRGINIA
CAROLINA
FLORIDÆ PARS
ERIE LAC
More of
Erieou
Castle
Eriech
ronons
Pohatan
Attiouandarons
APALACHE LACUS
Minquaas
Konekotays
Matunckonses
Capitanasses
Sauwanoos
Philadelphia
WEST
EAST
NEW JARSEY
Zurd Lac
Delaware Bay
THE NORTH SEA
MARE VIRGINIANUM anglice the SEA of VIRGINY
The Great of Chesapeake Bay
C. Charles
C. Henry
C. Hattaras
Stafford C.
Charles C.
Rappahanock C.
Kent C.
New Kent C.
Glofter C.
Henrico C.
City C.
Isle of Wight C.
Nansemond C.
Corotuk
ALBEMARLE COUNTY
Secotan
CLARENDON COUNTY
CRAVEN COUNTY
C. Feare
Milliaria Germanica

natives entirely out of the James-York peninsula, and ran a palisade across it. Some even began to settle boldly south of James and north of York.

Population, which had dropped to about a thousand by 1625, began to mount once more. Despite an even more savage war in 1644, in which five hundred settlers died, the English steadily outpeopled the Indians. By 1650 there were fifteen thousand Virginians.

Royal Colony

Meanwhile, the difficulties from which the colonists suffered gave King James the chance he had been waiting for. The king had never been very happy with the London Company. He did not like the liberal policies of its governing council, many of whom were members of the Parliament that was already beginning to rumble with revolt against Stuart rule. When word of the massacre and the starving condition of the colony reached England, James chose to blame the Company, saying it had failed to supply and defend its colonists adequately. The Company appealed to the House of Commons in a petition, calling Virginia "a child of the Kingdom, exposed in the wilderness," and asking for help. But the king blocked the move. On May 24, 1624, the charter of the London Company was revoked, and Virginia became a royal colony.

The first royal governor was Sir Francis Wyatt. He arrived without any instructions to assemble the House of Burgesses, and when the colonists petitioned the king to revive it, they were given only vague assurances of receiving "all such reasonable privileges as they have formerly enjoyed."

James died the year after the charter was revoked. His oldest son, for whom Henrico had been named, was already dead, so the succession went to James's second born, Charles. Charles I was more worldly than

An early map of the American colonies, showing Virginia's four great rivers and the Tidewater peninsulas between them.

his dour Scots father, but he had the same determination to get his own way. In a sense this was fortunate for Virginia, for the king's high-handedness brought him into such conflict with Parliament that he had little time for tampering with colonial affairs.

Charles permitted Virginia to convene an assembly in 1628, but only to authorize him to buy all their tobacco cheap. When they refused his price, he was angry but not angry enough—or strong enough—to do anything about it. He even allowed them to meet again the following year to consider systems of defense. And for the ten years following, his governors called the burgesses together every year on their own authority to settle local problems. They were years in which the governors themselves were in and out of trouble with the king and the Privy Council and their own colonial councils, and doubtless they were glad enough to let the people solve such minor questions by themselves. At last, in 1639, the distracted king gave his consent for the restoration of the general assembly of 1619 as a permanent institution in Virginia.

Organization

By that time, the quarrel between king and Parliament was coming to a head. The year that the last royal governor arrived, 1642, also saw the first battle of the English Civil War, which culminated in the unseating of the monarchy and the imprisonment and execution of the king. It was not until after the restoration of royal rule in 1660 that the home government paid close attention to Virginia again. Thus for thirty years, from 1630 to 1660, the colony was left virtually to herself—to work out forms of self-government and to establish patterns of life and culture of her own.

The colony was organized into eight counties, in which government was administered by judges of the county court. The court met once a month to try civil and criminal cases and to carry out such administrative functions as the planning of roads and bridges, the licensing of taverns, and the regulation of their prices. These justices served free, because a judgeship was considered a post of honor, but other county officers—the sheriff, the clerk, the lieutenant of the county militia—were paid. The sheriff's duties were to arrest suspected malefactors, to notify persons involved in lawsuits when they were to be present in court, and to collect taxes. The clerk kept records of the court's decisions, of wills, deeds, notes of indebtedness, and so on. Every able-bodied man from sixteen to sixty was supposed to serve in the militia—mostly in fighting Indians, although there was some fear of the Spanish in Florida, too—and the lieutenant commanded the unit from his district. All these officials were appointed by the governor, although he usually followed the recommendations of the local court.

Tobacco Economy

Tobacco dominated Virginian life. The price and quality of the leaf fluctuated widely from year to year, but it was still the staple cash crop of the colonial planter. It was the principal—often the only—form of

Transporting tobacco to market. Virginia's many creeks and rivers were useful, but if need be, the hogshead could become its own wagon.

currency. Taxes were paid in tobacco. Goods were bought with tobacco. Bets were laid in tobacco. Debts were discharged with tobacco. Fines were levied in tobacco. Tavern meals were paid for in tobacco. Militia officers and county officials took their salaries in tobacco. So did clergymen of the established church—sample fees: four hundred pounds for conducting a funeral, two hundred for performing a marriage service.

Methods of standardizing had to be developed. The cured hands of tobacco were shipped in a special type of barrel called a hogshead. Originally used for a wine or beer cask, the term hogshead as employed in the tobacco trade meant a crude wooden barrel, fashioned absolutely cylindrical, without any bulge in the middle, so that it could be tightly packed by a heavy press. It was put together without much skill or elaborate equipment, which made it an ideal container in the eyes of an isolated planter, dependent on himself or unskilled laborers. But a hogshead's crudeness was even more useful for tobacco inspectors, who could pull off a stave and examine the contents for "nesting"—hiding poor leaf under good.

In the early days, a hogshead might be small enough to hold a bare hundred pounds of leaf, but the standard hogshead gradually increased in size until it was eventually determined by legislative enactment that it was to weigh one thousand pounds.

It was the rolling of these hogsheads through the woods to the nearest navigable waterway—deep enough to float a shallow-draft cargo vessel—that formed the colony's first roads. Originally this was done by hand. Later, as the hogsheads grew large and the distances to water greater, horses were used. Planters simply fastened shafts to the hogshead itself—reinforced with "tires" of hickory—and hitched up two animals in tandem. Sometimes all the planters of a certain district would meet on a set day and travel to the embarkation point in caravan.

Easy as tobacco was to raise, the plant had one drawback: It wore out the soil very rapidly. The first year's crop on newly cleared land was likely to be a big one, though the leaf was seldom of the highest quality. For a few succeeding years, crops would be smaller but of

A two-story house of squared logs, shutters in place of window glass—typical of many early Virginia houses.

better grade, but thereafter the field yielded increasingly poorer and smaller crops. Planters were always looking for new land, importing servants as much for their headrights as for their services, pushing out to the frontier, spreading farther and farther apart. As a result, the colony slowly developed into a land of large farms, with few towns and those far apart. This in turn made it necessary for a plantation to become self-sufficient.

Plantation Life, 1650's

A small farmer, owning perhaps a few hundred acres, probably lived in a brick or clapboard version of the log cabin—a one-room house, usually fourteen to sixteen feet long. People had begun to abandon thatched roofs, because with wood so plentiful it was easier to roof with boards or shingle—or bark, like Indian dwellings—so the smallholder's house probably had a roof of shakes. A large chimney of brick stuck out—often far out—at one end. The floor was probably clay or pun-

The Adam Thoroughgood house, built between 1636 and 1640, is typical of a prosperous smallholder's dwelling.

cheon—halved logs laid with the flat side up. The windows, few and small, were casement affairs, that is, they opened out like doors and were closed either with wooden shutters or with leaded casements filled with thick, diamond-latticed glass. At the end opposite the chimney was a stair or ladder to the garret, where the family slept. In time, the owner might add on an extra room to the back of this house, under an extension of the roof. This gave the house a lopsided look, like a New England saltbox house, and the extended roof was called a catslide. Perhaps the planter and his family moved their sleeping quarters to the addition while the new bond servant—his passage paid in tobacco—took over their old quarters in the garret.

The smallholder would have several outbuildings as well: some kind of shed for his cattle, a smokehouse where his hams and bacons were salted down, perhaps a small smithy where he could repair his tools, and, of course, a curing house for his tobacco. Smokehouse and forge would probably be sod-roofed because of the danger from fire to wooden roofs. He would probably have a small orchard, a vegetable garden, a planting of flax. His worn-out tobacco fields would still bear corn or even wheat, or he might have turned them into cow pastures. He would certainly have a well near the house, and in the early days—or if he was settled on the frontier—he would have erected *pallyzados* around the farmyard.

Beyond this protection would lie the woods and the newly cleared fields, many still showing their fresh stumps, where his "green gold" was growing, the tobacco that had brought him to the New World in the first place.

His richer next-door neighbor—settled perhaps as close as five miles from the smallholder—lived much the same life though on a somewhat grander scale. His house, for instance, probably had two stories plus a garret. There would be two great chimneys, one at either end, and the large ground floor would be divided into great room, or hall, and parlor. The planter would conduct his business, interview his servants or ships' captains, trade with Indians in his great room, while family life was lived in the comparative privacy of the parlor. The stairs might be at the back of the hall or the owner might add on a special tower, called a "stair case," to contain the stairs. His casement windows would certainly have glass panes, possibly set in decorative patterns. His roof might have Dutch gables and nonflammable pantiles, and his chimney would be finished off with ornamental brickwork. Life was secure enough for him to think of prettying it up.

He would have many more outbuildings than his neighbor, because he was running a much larger and more complex operation. There would be quarters for his dozen or more servants—most of them indentured whites but probably a black slave or two as well—and a house for his overseer, who was perhaps a bond servant himself. No physician was likely to be within call, so in addition to a kitchen garden, he would probably have a garden of herbs, the only medicines he knew, for dosing his family and servants: calendula, nasturtium, foxglove, yarrow,

A tobacco wharf. The annual crop was assembled here for shipment to England in the tobacco fleet.

spearmint, violet, crocus, probably many plants learned from Indians, too. He might even have a pleasure garden, called a hortyard.

He might have a brewhouse, a bakehouse, a spinning-and-weaving house, a tanning house, a fair-sized stable, a dairy, a sawmill, a warehouse for his packed hogsheads and other goods. If his plantation was situated on the James itself or the York, he might have a private wharf where the tobacco ships could tie up and load at their ease. If not, he would at least have a shed where he kept a flatboat with which to transport his crop to the central wharves where the annual crop was assembled.

There might be special buildings of many kinds, because the seventeenth-century Virginian had a mercantile turn of mind and was often willing to engage in a number of sidelines. William Byrd I, founder of one of Virginia's most illustrious families, made much of his money importing bond servants and selling them to other planters at a profit. A large plantation might run a cooperage or a gristmill or a boatbuilding operation, selling the products to neighbors or shipping them to England. A lively trade in deer hides had sprung up with the Indians; deer hide, being lighter and finer than cowhide, was much in demand in Europe for workmen's breeches, jackets, and aprons. An energetic planter might also have gangs of men out making pitch and tar or cutting cedar shingles to ship along with his hogsheads.

But it was still those hogsheads of tobacco on which he chiefly relied. And the more fields of it he had, the larger and larger his estate spread, the richer he grew. Profits from other ventures went into land and servants with which to grow tobacco. If his poorer neighbor found he could not compete with this large enterprise next door, he might sell out his holdings to the richer man and move to the frontier. As the century went on, the rich got much richer.

Governor Sir William Berkeley—a gallant, irascible old tyrant who defied Parliament to proclaim Charles II king.

The Coming of the Commonwealth

The troubles in England did not leave Virginia wholly unaffected. Charles I's last appointed governor, Sir William Berkeley, was a staunch royalist. When news came that the monarch had been beheaded, Sir William's first act was to persuade the Assembly to condemn those "treaterous proceedings" and to declare the nineteen-year-old Prince of Wales Charles II, king in Virginia if not in England.

Sir William was popular in the colony in those early years. He had brought tax relief to poor settlers—partly by sacrificing some of his own salary—had assented to a law that prohibited taxation without the consent of the House of Burgesses, and had likewise agreed that the representatives should be immune from arrest while the House was sitting. He also allowed men convicted in the county courts to appeal to the Assembly for review of their cases. Since the county judgeships were apt to be distributed to rich men who could afford to serve free, this was an important concession to the poor and defenseless.

Consequently, when war vessels of the Parliament arrived in 1652 to subdue the colony, they found a governor without enemies, and the most they could do was unseat him. He retired to his plantation, Green Spring near Jamestown, and the choice of governor was left in the hands of the Assembly. Early in 1660, suspecting that the monarchy was about to be restored, the Assembly elected Sir William Berkeley.

Population Growth

But the Virginia of 1660 was different from the Virginia of 1630, even from the Virginia of 1649. It was during these years that most of Virginia's great families arrived—the Lees, the Beverleys, the Randolphs, the Carters, the Pages, and so forth. From fifteen thousand in 1650 the population had swelled in ten years to an estimated forty thousand. Most of these were persons displaced by the Civil War: Scots and English prisoners, shipped over by the victorious Cromwell to get them out of the way; later, fugitives from the wrath of the about-to-be-restored king, or simply men impoverished by the conflict and seeking a new life. Possibly included among the latter class (the family manor was sold three years after he left it) was the son of an old Northamptonshire family, who arrived in 1657 and settled on Bridges Creek–by name, John Washington.

Desperately as labor was needed by the established planters, they could not assimilate this much this fast. The overrun swarmed to the new lands at the edge of the settlements and pushed the frontiers rapidly north, south, west, displacing still more Indians. Upcountry farms did not produce as fine a tobacco as that of Tidewater, but it was good enough for the Dutch, who for some reason liked their tobacco coarse and harsh. Soon these newcomers were sending the total production figures for tobacco up and up and up. And just at a time when the restored king was introducing a new mercantile system.

New Colonial Policy

In 1660 the British Empire in the Western Hemisphere consisted of many little settlements scattered about the Atlantic Ocean–a handful on Chesapeake Bay and the Virginia rivers, a sprinkling along the New England coast, some sugar islands in the Caribbean. The only thing that could tie these elements together into an economic and political unit was domination of the sea. Charles II was determined above everything else to acquire a strong navy and a prosperous merchant marine. Almost his first actions as king were to get a tough Navigation Act passed by Parliament and to open a sea war with the Dutch for control of the carrying trade.

Before 1660, planters had been accustomed to selling their tobacco wherever it brought the best prices and shipping it in vessels that offered the lowest freight charges. Often, even for good Tidewater leaf, that meant north European markets and Dutch bottoms (ships). Now the Navigation Act prohibited colonists from exporting their products or importing their necessities in anything but English or colonial ships and from buying or selling certain products to any country but England. Foremost among the "enumerated articles" was tobacco.

Since there were many Virginians selling tobacco and only a few Englishmen buying it—many of them favorites of the king, granted special monopolies—the buyers could just about set their own prices. Hardest hit of all, of course, were the poor newcomers on the frontier, then at the fall line of the rivers. Even the doughty old royalist Sir William Berkeley was moved to protest the new system:

"We cannot but resent that forty thousand people should be impoverished to enrich little more than forty merchants, who . . . indeed have forty thousand servants in us at cheaper rates than other men have slaves."

The system did have some two-way features. A bounty was paid for certain products, like naval stores. The English were forbidden to grow tobacco or other colonial products (tobacco *could* be grown in Europe as far north as Moscow), and the shipping provisions were a shot in the arm for those colonies that depended heavily on the sea. But for Virginia it was a disaster, bringing immediate and widespread hardship.

The Assembly passed laws to limit tobacco production, but the neighboring colonies—Maryland and later Carolina—always refused to pass similar legislation, and Virginia could not enforce restrictions alone. The planters themselves, from lack of foresight, evaded the laws. And, in any case, the Virginia enactments were ultimately disallowed by the king. Whatever the price paid for the leaf itself, the customs duty per pound remained high. Charles did not care what the planters suffered as long as he got his share.

To make matters worse, Sir William Berkeley turned crusty and pigheaded—and, it was said, avaricious—in his old age. In his relations with the home government Sir William continued to fight valiantly for the good of the colony, battling off attempts by Charles to give away enormous portions of Virginia's territory, pleading the planters' cause to the monarch in person, rallying the people to fight back when bold Dutch men-of-war attacked the tobacco fleet in Chesapeake Bay itself. But in his relations with the common people of Virginia, he became arbitrary and tyrannical.

Local offices were bestowed on favorites of his, who were allowed to defraud men of money and justice. Taxes were heavy and unfairly distributed. The House of Burgesses, which sat for fifteen long years without new elections, was filled with supporters of the governor. The people—who looked back on the eight years of the Commonwealth as a time when they had known true self-rule—now found themselves without a voice.

Poverty and oppression—Virginia was ripe for an insurrection. No one realized it more certainly than the old governor himself. "How miserable that man is," he wrote just before the deluge broke, "that Governes a People wher six parts of seaven at least are Poore Endebted Discontented and Armed."

CHAPTER FOUR

Now Jagg, Ragg & Bobtayle Carry a High Hand

Insurrection began with an Indian uprising in the summer of 1675. Whites, avenging the death of a white man, set upon a party of Susquehannock Indians, probably not the ones who had killed their friend, and murdered fourteen of them. Later, parleying with another group from the same tribe, they butchered the envoys before the eyes of their own people. In revenge, the outraged Susquehannocks spread out across the Maryland and Virginia backcountry, bringing war of a chilling new sort.

For the Susquehannocks were supplied with guns and powder—traded to them by the governor and his appointees for profitable otter and beaver pelts—and knew how to use them with skill. Moreover, they were of an Iroquoisan culture, closely related to that of the Five Nations, which meant that they practiced torture on their captives.

Early in 1676 they raided plantations on the upper parts of the Potomac and Rappahannock rivers and massacred thirty-six settlers, some by burning or flaying alive. The survivors fled in mortal terror and gathered in hastily erected fortifications, sending to the government for help. Governor Berkeley raised a force of troops to march against the Indians, but just as they were about to set out, he arbitrarily changed his mind and ordered the men to disband. He gave no reason for this, but in the aftermath of his inaction, three hundred more Virginian murders were reported that winter.

In March, the Berkeley-dominated Assembly met to consider the defense of the frontier. It was decided to establish a line of forts at the "heads," or falls, of the rivers, to be paid for with new and heavy taxes.

These forts were to be garrisoned with troops, but the soldiers were prohibited from firing on the Indians or marching out against their villages without special permission from the governor.

King Philip's War was raging just then in New England, and the governor feared to provoke a general, continent-wide uprising against all English settlements; moreover, it was his policy to keep the peaceful and submissive Pamunkey Indians as a buffer between the white frontier and the warlike Susquehannocks. So there was reason for his proceeding with caution.

But the embittered people could not take the long view. "No bullits [must] pierse beaver skins!" they cried and declared the forts "a great grievance, juggle, and cheat."

The seething commoners were eager to take matters into their own hands. When rumors spread that large bodies of Indians were gathering along the upper James—and this only a few weeks after the March Assembly meeting—they flocked together in an armed mob at Jordan's Point, on the south bank of the James (near modern Hopewell). They lacked only a leader. Suddenly, after the overseer of a plantation at Henrico was killed, they found such a man in the overseer's master. His name was Nathaniel Bacon, Jr.

Young Bacon

Bacon had come to Virginia in 1673 at the age of twenty-six. He was a small, slim, black-haired young man, described as being "of an ominous, pensive, melancholly Aspect," but capable of decisive action under pressure, as he was soon to prove. He had left England under something of a cloud, having been removed from Cambridge for extravagance, caught out in an attempted fraud, and caused his wife to be disinherited for marrying him. But he was welcomed in Virginia, where his cousin, Nathaniel Bacon, Sr., was a member of Governor Berkeley's Council. After a few months he was appointed to the Council himself. He settled at "Curles Neck" in Henrico County, about forty miles up the river from Jamestown, and soon acquired a second plantation called Bacon's

Quarter within the present city of Richmond. This latter area was then at the edge of settlement, and it was here that the overseer had been killed.

Roused, Bacon crossed the James with some friends and appeared among the volunteer soldiers. As soon as they saw him coming—a gentleman, a member of the Council, actually paying attention to their problems at last!—they set up a shout, "Bacon! Bacon!"

The young councillor had no commission to "array" militia. The issuing of such authorizations was a jealously guarded prerogative of the governor. But Bacon's vanity was not proof against such a clamor. He agreed to lead the volunteers. They signed a round robin, "writing their names circular wise, that the ring-leaders might not be found out," recrossed the James, and set out for New Kent County to the north to enlist additional men.

Before he left Jordan's Point, Bacon had taken the elementary precaution of notifying the governor of his action and requesting a formal commission. The news enraged Sir William. He proclaimed Bacon and his followers "rebells and mutineers" who would be pardoned only if they instantly laid down their arms. Then he lost no time hastening upriver after the hotheaded young councillor. But by that time Bacon and his men were deep into Pamunkey territory, scattering the innocent tribes, then heading west and south along the traders' path on the trail of the Susquehannocks.

After a long detour through the territory of the neutral Nottoway and Meherrin Indians, in an unsuccessful attempt to enlist their aid, Bacon and his men reached the Roanoke River. Here, near the present city of Clarksville, on the North Carolina border, the volunteer soldiers came on a strongly fortified village of the Occaneechees, located on an island in the river. The Occaneechees were wary. They reported that the Susquehannocks were indeed in the vicinity, entrenched a few miles away, and offered to go capture them, but they made it plain that the Virginians were not particularly welcome in the region either.

Bacon's men had exhausted both themselves and their provisions during their hundred-mile trek through the forest, but the Occaneechees refused to succor them. (Perhaps they could not—spring, after winter stores have been consumed, is the hungriest time of year for a subsistence economy.) Their offer to attack the Susquehannocks was accepted, however, and carried out successfully.

Bacon could then be said to have completed his campaign—tracked down his enemy and, if not defeated him, saw someone else do so. Still, the Virginians lingered near the river. Stories differ as to why. Bacon has been accused of wanting to seize £1,000 worth of beaver pelts stored in the village (although how he could have transported such a load all the way home without a string of packponies is not explained); other accounts say that the volunteers were too desperate for food to venture on the long return journey; possibly they just wanted to kill some Indians.

In any event, after a two-day wait, Bacon's men waded out to the island and, when one of their number was shot, used that as an excuse for

Governor Berkeley's estate, Green Spring, near Jamestown.

an attack on the Occaneechees. Closing in on the Indian fort in the night, the Virginians fired through the portholes with deadly effect, slaying men, women, and children.

This "battle" won, Bacon marched his men back to Henrico.

Jamestown Is Threatened

Meanwhile, Governor Berkeley, while "in the upper parts to wait Bacon's return," was beginning to realize how hot the people's anger flamed, that his failure to act in the Indian crisis was only a symbol to them of their deeper grievances. He issued a second proclamation against Bacon May 10, removing him from the Council and again urging his followers to abandon him. But on the same day, to appease the angry commoners, he dissolved the long-sitting Assembly and ordered new elections. He then returned to his plantation at Green Spring to await their outcome.

To his chagrin he found that Bacon and his men were widely admired as heroes and saviors of the colony, even among people not living in exposed settlements. From all sides poor men "but lately crept out of the condition of Servants" were nominated to the House. Scarcely eight members were supporters of the governor, and to represent Henrico County, people chose Nathaniel Bacon himself and his close friend James Crews.

Bacon's followers were so afraid that Berkeley might have their idol seized or assassinated that they kept a watch around his house. He himself wrote a straightforward letter to the governor, expressing loyalty and submission to his authority but not apologizing for his actions against the Indians. However, when he set out for Jamestown to take his seat for the June 5 opening session of the House, he proceeded with extreme caution.

Not extreme enough, as it turned out, for the governor's forces cornered the sloop in which he had descended the river and carried him before Sir William a prisoner.

The old man threw up his hands. "Now I behold the greatest rebell that ever was in Virginia!" he cried. But a few moments later he offered to let Bacon go free on parole—that is, if he gave his word as a gentleman not to try to escape. When Bacon agreed and expressed thanks at this generous treatment, Berkeley told him that if he would make a public admission of his disobedience he would receive a full pardon and be restored to his Council seat.

The governor was not being foolishly magnanimous. A good two thousand of Bacon's followers had crowded into town as soon as they heard of his arrest, and there were angry rumblings in the streets of Jamestown.

Two days later, on his knees before the burgesses and the Council, Nathaniel Bacon handed over his written submission. The governor spoke of sinners that repenteth and repeated three times, "God forgive you, I forgive you." It was done. The following day, the black-haired young man was restored to his Council seat, and shortly thereafter he was promised a "Commission to Gett voluntiers to Goe against the Indians."

First Seizure of Jamestown

That should have ended the matter. Perhaps if the commission had been granted, it would have. But the all-important papers did not arrive, and after a day or two Bacon and his friends began to suspect that the promise was nothing but a ruse to get his frontier followers to leave Jamestown. Taking alarm, he slipped quietly out of town and returned to Henrico.

There, men flocked around Bacon, asking him if he had received the promised commission to lead them. When he had to say no, they were enraged at this insult to their hero—and to their own newfound power—and they vowed to follow him back to Jamestown and either get the commission or "pull downe the Towne."

On June 23, Bacon stormed into the capital at the head of six hundred armed and ragged men. The stouthearted old governor had tried to prevent this invasion, but he could get so few volunteers to man the

The old governor confronts the young rebel before the Statehouse in Jamestown: "Here, shoot me!"

defenses that it seemed safer to offer no resistance to Bacon's angry followers than to risk being defeated. Bacon quickly took over the town, stationing guards at the ferry and fort and drawing up the rest of the men before the statehouse.

Jamestown in 1676 was hardly bigger or more populous than the village of 1619, but the shabby wattle-and-daub huts had been replaced by substantial brick buildings two stories or more high. However, many of these houses were empty, owned by councillors or burgesses and occupied only during sessions of the Assembly. The Statehouse, built in 1662, was one of a handsome row of houses facing the river and contained large and well-appointed rooms for the Council, the House of Burgesses, and other colonial officials.

Inside this building the frightened legislators now conferred hastily with the governor. Berkeley sent a messenger to find out what Bacon wanted and was told a commission as general of all volunteers against the Indians. Under pressure from the burgesses and councillors, Berkeley produced such a paper, but in the meantime Bacon had changed his mind. Now he wanted a commission as general of *all forces in Virginia* against the Indians—the equivalent of demanding military control of the colony.

In a passion of rage, Berkeley stormed out of the Statehouse and denounced Bacon in the presence of his men as a rebel and traitor. Crying out that he would cut off his hands rather than sign such a document, he tore open his coat and presented his breast. "Here! Shoot me! 'Fore God, fair mark, shoot!"

Bacon ignored this offer, saying he had not come to harm a hair of the governor's head, and Sir William stalked back into the building, where his advisers begged him to pacify the invaders with the paper they wanted.

Meanwhile, Bacon cooled his heels in the street, strutting to and fro, swearing "new-coyned oaths." When a group of burgesses collected at a window to peek out at him, he ordered his men to present their cocked firelocks. "Damn my blood, I'll kill Governor, Council, Assembly, and all!" he shouted.

"For God's sake, hold your hands and forbear a little," one burgess cried, fluttering a handkerchief, "and you shall have what you please."

Finally, after much "hurrying, solicitation, and importunity" from all sides, Sir William yielded and granted the commission Bacon wanted.

But now *that* was not enough either. On the day following, Bacon was back with new demands—blank commissions for subordinate officers of the new general's choice, dismissal from office of certain followers of the governor, letters to the king justifying Bacon's past and present conduct. The humiliated governor gave him what he wanted, hoping only to be rid of him and his turbulent followers. "Now, tagg, ragg & bobtayle carry a high hand," wrote one disdainful witness.

And while these arrangements were being made, some of the burgesses thought to please the Baconians by reading to them some of the new measures that had been enacted during the session. A liberal, reforming spirit had activated the House, and they had passed laws extending the vote, curbing the powers of the governor's appointees, removing the exemption of councillors from taxation. But when they appeared with the papers in their hands, the rough, illiterate men rose up "like a swarme of bees" and shouted, "No laws! We will have no laws!"

Mobs seldom understand true reform.

The Governor Flees

The Assembly completed its work on Sunday, June 25, 1676. That morning, news came that Indians had killed eight more colonists only twenty-three miles from Jamestown. The alarmed frontiersmen were then only too anxious to leave for home. Employing his new commission, Bacon ordered supplies sent upriver to the falls, and the next morning flags were unfurled, drums sounded, and he marched away at the head of his troops. Sir William Berkeley witnessed his departure in wrathful silence.

Bacon's commission, however illegally obtained, strengthened his position among men who had before hesitated to follow him. Now recruits flocked in, and his appointed officers rode where they pleased, seizing horses, supplies, and arms. Naturally the rich planters were their chief target. In July a group of them in Gloucester County petitioned Berkeley for assistance against these confiscations, and the governor took this to mean that the tide had turned against Bacon.

He crossed the York and rode about trying to win volunteers, saying that Bacon's move south would leave the northern counties exposed to Indian attack. But Berkeley had miscalculated. The move was seen only as an attempt to stab Bacon in the back while he, still a popular hero, was "advanceing against the common enimy." Few recruits appeared.

The news of Berkeley's move reached Bacon just as he was about to leave the falls on his march south. Calling his men together by beat of drum, he stood up and made an indignant speech: "Gentlemen and fellow soldiers, the governor is now in Gloucester County endeavoring to raise forces against us, having declared us rebels and traitors. . . . Let us descend to know . . . why . . . those whom they have raised for their Defence . . . they should thus seek to destroy!"

A great shout rose from the soldiers: "We are all ready to die in the field rather than be hanged like rogues!"

But there was to be no battle. As soon as Berkeley heard that Bacon had reversed himself and was marching north, he fled across Chesapeake Bay to the Eastern Shore, leaving the whole of Tidewater Virginia in the rebels' power.

Conference at Middle Plantation

The secret of Bacon's success was the control he maintained over his men. Although he commissioned them to seize military supplies from civilians, he did not permit them to loot and destroy. Consequently his actions carried an air of order and authority. When he summoned a general meeting of planters at Middle Plantation, a site along the old palisade halfway between the James and York rivers, many men of substance showed up.

Bacon presented them with a proclamation denouncing Berkeley as having acted against the king's interest and in effect declaring him and his "pernitious Councellors" outlaws. Then he read aloud to them an oath he had framed, which bound them to aid in the Indian war, to oppose the governor, and—until the king had heard their grievances—to resist any troops that might be sent from England.

Many of the planters feared to take so brazen an oath, particularly that part about opposing the king's own troops. But Bacon locked the door of the meeting place and, partly by threats, partly by his "specious and subtill pretences," induced them to sign. Among the signers were some of the most prominent men in the colony.

That done, Bacon dispatched two of his lieutenants in a captured English merchant ship to the Eastern Shore to seize Governor Berkeley, whom he proposed to send to England for trial. Then he himself went back to chasing Indians again, this time the peaceful and inoffensive Pamunkeys. After a long pursuit, he cornered them in a swamp, attacked, and when they offered no resistance contented himself with killing only eight or so. He returned to the James with forty-five captives and much pitiful booty—mats, bags, parcels of wampum.

It was the high point of his rebellion, for when he reached the settlements again, he was informed that Governor Berkeley was once more in possession of Jamestown.

Second Seizure of Jamestown

The two officers he had sent to capture Sir William had bungled the job. With the help of some of Berkeley's friends, the English captain had retaken his own ship. The governor had embarked in this vessel from the Eastern Shore, accompanied by as many loyal recruits and gentlemen as he could muster, in sloops, and had occupied the capital before those rebels left in town could organize a defense.

Bacon set out for the town at once and on September 13 reached Green Spring, three miles away. So far he had been unopposed, but he knew that fighting lay ahead. His first seizure of Jamestown had been as much by surprise as by force. Now it would have to be by force. He gathered his men together in a field and harangued them spiritedly.

"Come on, my hearts of gold," he finished on a high note, "he that dies in the field lies in the bed of honor!"

Outside Jamestown, Bacon drew up his men in an old Indian field. The only approach to the city was by way of a narrow isthmus, which Berkeley had fortified with a palisade and three cannon. Moreover, several ships were so disposed that their guns covered these defenses. Bacon made a personal reconnoiter of the works, hoping to goad the governor into sending his forces out after him. When that didn't work, Bacon set his men to digging earthworks as a counter fortification.

Two axes and a spade were the men's only tools, and after a night of labor the ditch was still incomplete. Bacon was desperate. He sent out squadrons of men to round up the wives of as many of the gover-

After his third capture of Jamestown, rebel Nathaniel Bacon burns the city and rides out against the governor.

nor's supporters as he could find; then he lined these women up in front of his men as a living shield while they completed their work. He also displayed some of his Indian captives—"proof" that he had been out protecting the frontier while the governor was elsewhere.

On September 15, the earthworks ready, Bacon released the ladies. Instantly, a signal was given, and the loyalists opened up with musketry from the palisade and heavy shot from the ships' guns. But Bacon's men, protected by their ditch, were not harmed. On the following day, a watchman Bacon had stationed on a nearby chimney called down that the governor's forces were making ready to sally out. The rebels braced themselves.

But the governor commanded few enthusiastic followers. They, "like scholers goeing to schoole, went out with hevie harts, but returned hom with light heeles." When Bacon produced three cannon the next day and set systematically to mounting them, the loyalists gave up. They spiked their own guns and, slipping away in the night, abandoned Jamestown to the victorious rebels.

Temporarily, at any rate. Governor Berkeley would not let his little command sail away altogether but lingered in the river to see what would happen. What happened was that Jamestown went up in flames.

The Rebellion Disintegrates

Bacon had heard that loyalist forces were being enlisted in the north to come down against him. Not wanting to get caught between them and the governor's ships, he had destroyed the town and marched out. These new troops dissolved as fast as he approached, as had all the others enlisted to fight him. But the approach was not very fast, for Bacon had fallen desperately ill of dysentery. Late in October he died, and his body was secretly buried.

The rebellion rapidly disintegrated after that. Pockets of resistance remained under other leaders, and some skirmishes were even won, prolonging the insurrection through December, 1676. But now anarchy was abroad. Toward the end, even Bacon had begun to lose control of his wild frontiersmen, who had seen no reason not to plunder and rob the rich supporters of their enemy. Now rebel bands wandered about, making little pretense of defending the frontier, of demanding reform. They ran off cattle, took fence rails for firewood, even invaded houses and wantonly destroyed furnishings.

The colony had had enough. Sympathy for the rebels faded, and several of the most important surrendered. By mid-January it was safe for Sir William to return to the mainland.

The old governor–born the year before Jamestown was founded, first appointed to his office before Nathaniel Bacon was born, now seventy years old with some twenty-six years of service to Virginia to his credit–had been cut to the quick by his humiliation. Why, Virginians had once voluntarily chosen him for his office! How dared these upstart newcomers mistreat the king's viceroy in such fashion? He set out on an orgy of revenge.

Those rebel leaders he could lay his hands on immediately he rushed to trial and execution, often within the day. At least one such man—William Drummond, a wealthy planter who had supported the cause of reform—may have been drawn and quartered, and his mutilated body posted at public places as a ghastly warning to future rebels. A few lucky rebels were never found. The estates of others were confiscated, their widows and children turned out to starve. To reimburse himself for his financial losses, Berkeley resorted to outright extortion, forcing men whose rebel connections had not even been proved to impoverish themselves in order to be released from prison or threat of hanging.

When King Charles heard of the extent of Berkeley's acts of vengeance, he remarked in disgust, "That old fool has hanged more men in that naked country than I have done for the murder of my father!"

On January 29, 1677, an English fleet appeared in the James. It was carrying English troops and brought news that Sir William Berkeley was to be superseded as governor of Virginia.

CHAPTER FIVE

Souls! Damn Your Souls! Make Tobacco!

King Charles II was no fool. He knew so widespread an uprising could only have been fomented by mismanagement somewhere. Along with soldiers to restore order, he sent a commission to investigate the entire affair. But so powerful was the newly reseated governor and his faction that not even the king's own representatives could regain control of the wretched province. Even after Berkeley sailed, which was not for five months, his followers continued to thwart and insult the commissioners and intimidate those who tried to report the grievances that had driven Bacon and his men to such extremes. The old governor had hardly landed in England before he took to his bed and died, and his brother raised a further uproar in the Privy Council itself, accusing the commissioners of murdering him.

The new governor, Lord Culpeper, did not bother to appear until 1680—and then only under direct threats from the king—remained only four months, returned again briefly in 1682, then went back to England for good. He was replaced by Lord Howard of Effingham, who was more conscientious but also a harder man all around. He had orders to collect quitrents—small but permanent payments due on purchased land, a holdover from feudalism—from all Virginia holdings, and he proceeded to do so ruthlessly.

For Virginia all this meant years of tyranny and disorder and poverty. In the 1670's and 1680's, the Assembly was systematically stripped of many previously granted rights: the right to hear judicial appeals, the right to elect their own clerk (so that a governor's "spy" might be placed in the burgesses' midst), the right to control all revenues.

By bitter experience, Virginians learned of the importance of the taxing power. The burgesses did not surrender these rights lightly but battled tooth and nail to save something from the wreck. Because of their efforts, the House at least retained the right to initiate legislation and kept some control over general taxes. And in the dogged fight to secure these remnants, Virginians developed powerful political skills.

The Glorious Revolution

Charles died in 1685 and was succeeded by his Roman Catholic brother, James II—a mulishly shortsighted man even by the standards of a family famed for obstinacy. He was dethroned in 1688 and replaced by his Protestant daughter Mary and her Dutch husband, William Prince of Orange. William and Mary were the first monarchs to acknowledge publicly and in writing the supremacy of Parliament. Their Declaration of Rights, among other things, denied the right of any king to suspend laws passed by Parliament or to exact money without its consent. Eight decades later, Americans were to remind Englishmen of this principle in slightly different words: "Taxation without representation is tyranny."

But for the moment all Virginians hoped for was to get rid of Lord Howard of Effingham. The new rulers did not quite remove him, but they did recall him to England and send Francis Nicholson as lieutenant governor in his place.

Nicholson was famous for having a volcanic temper, but for all that he turned out to be an administrator of experience and ability, genuinely interested in the people of Virginia. He toured the frontier, inspected the colony's defenses—both against Indians and against the depredations of pirates—and promoted religion and education. He liked to invite prominent citizens to dine at his home, which was a modest one, and discuss improvements for the colony. He made himself popular with the sports-loving Virginians by instituting public athletic contests—although he confined these "Olympick Games" to "the better sort of Virginians onely." When a subscription was taken up to found a

A tobacco plantation. A hand of tobacco lies on the ground while slaves labor to fill empty hogsheads.

college in the colony, he was the first to give—£150 out of his own purse.

Chattel Slavery

Nicholson's coming coincided with a turn for the better in the colony's economy. The market for tobacco had begun to expand, and a cheaper way of producing it had been discovered: slavery.

One object of Charles II's sea wars had been to wrest a share of the slave trade away from the Dutch. Soon the African Company was established on that continent and trading with chieftains for their captives in war. Most of these victims went to the sugar islands, but more and more of the slavers had begun to visit the Chesapeake.

In 1671 Virginia had a servant population of six thousand indentured whites and two thousand Negro slaves to forty thousand or more freemen. But planters were growing disenchanted with the use of bond servants. Now many of these bondmen were "transportees"—convicts whose sentences had been commuted from death to transportation to the colonies—and although they represented the less hardened element among English convicts, they were nonetheless a comedown from the voluntary immigrant. Moreover, many whites died of the "seasoning fever" within the first year of purchase, and even if a man lived out the whole of his servitude (a convict usually served seven years as against four for a bondman), that was barely enough time to train him to his work. A black slave, now—he was much more expensive to buy than a white man, but you had him for life and his children after him. By 1700, black tobacco workers outnumbered whites.

Because a slave was so expensive—£60 to £80 as compared with about £12 for a white bond servant—only a comparatively well-off man could afford one to begin with. The more slaves a man had, the richer he grew; the richer he grew, the more slaves he could buy. It was a vicious circle.

Cultivating the Crop

Over the years planters had developed more efficient methods of tobacco cultivation. Now, instead of being sown broadcast as John Gerard had recommended, tobacco seed was first soaked for two or three days in milk or stale beer, then mixed with earth and set aside in a warm place until the sprouts appeared. Meanwhile, the patches, or beds, were being prepared. A tobacco patch was never plowed. A farmer might simply burn brush over the land he intended to sow, then hoe in the ashes. Another technique was to fertilize with the droppings of doves or swine (but not that of cattle—"cowpen tobacco" was thought to have a very strong flavor). When the plants were large enough, the seedlings were set out in hills, kept carefully weeded, and, if the weather was dry, watered daily just after sundown.

When the plants reached a full two feet, they were topped, as in John

LIFE IN EASTERN VIRGINIA.
The Home of the Planter.

Rolfe's day. (A few plants were allowed to form seeds for the following year's crop, but not many were needed–tobacco was and is one of the most prolific seed-producing plants in the world.) After topping, the plant would put forth suckers near the base of the leaves, and these had to be carefully pruned or they would sap the strength of the parent plant. The field gangs were obliged to keep watch over the growing leaf for tobacco worms. On some plantations, a border of mustard was sown around a tobacco seedbed; the fly pests preferred mustard to tobacco and would feed on it instead.

The crop was harvested in September, the entire plant being cut off near the ground. The stalk was pierced and strung with four or five other plants upside down on a "tobacco stick"—a pine lath about four feet long. These sticks were hung on scaffolds in the sun for a day or two, then taken inside the tobacco house to be cured.

A Virginia tobacco house was not quite like any other farm structure anywhere. It was constructed of unchinked, loosely joined logs, was square in floor plan, and stood half again as tall as it was wide. Often two such sheds were built side by side, with space between them for a wagon to be driven in and out, and common roof over all. Upright timbers, four feet apart, formed racks to hold the four-foot tobacco sticks, which were mounted to the ceiling in carefully staggered order, so that air could circulate freely.

The floor was of clay. If the weather was damp and there was danger that the crop would not dry out properly, fires were lighted, five feet or so apart, of low heat at first but gradually hotting up as the leaves turned color. Pungent hickory was the usual fuel, although some planters preferred sassafras or sweet-gum wood. During the drying process, the crudely constructed building gave off smoke from every chink and all the fields were overhung with haze. But normally the crop was simply left to age, usually until the following spring.

When the tobacco had reached just the right stage (not too dark, not too light, not too moist, not too dry, not too cold, not too warm), it was "struck"—taken down from the racks, the leaves gently stripped from the stalks, sorted out into various grades, and tied up into bunches of eight to twelve leaves called hands. A discarded leaf, twisted around the stems of the hand, bound it together. The hands were then piled up, pressed, and packed into hogsheads for shipment.

Plantation Life, 1690's

A tobacco grower's life was lived in the 1690's much as it had been forty years earlier, except perhaps that the planter had added wings onto his hall-and-parlor house or extended it by a few feet at either end to make his chimneys flush with the outer wall of the building; sticking-out chimneys were going out of style. Perhaps he might have imported some of the newfangled sash windows from London—that is, windows that slid up and down in their frames like modern ones—and enlarged his window openings to contain them. These new windows, their panes filled with clear plate glass, would let in much more light and air than the old leaded casements. Perhaps too much light for the Virginia climate; perhaps the planter also added louvered shutters to be closed against the hot July sun. And, of course, beyond the house and its immediate outbuildings there would be a lengthening street of cabins—probably log cabins, for this mode of construction had finally been introduced to Virginia—where his black tobacco gangs lived.

The rich planter had probably begun to order frills from the London merchant to whom his tobacco had been consigned: fancy furniture, books, silks, articles of silver, and perhaps a chest of that strange new substance from China called tea. (At first, his wife might have been confused about how to prepare it. Some American housewives boiled it up like spinach, threw out the water, and served the leaves with butter and salt.) Many planters were so eager for these little luxuries that they bought them on credit, piling up debts which they—and sometimes their descendents—could never seem to get clear of.

What had happened to this man's smallholder neighbor? Throughout the colonial period the smallholder, working a hundred to seven hundred acres, represented the majority of Virginia's population. He could ably hold his own, making up in the quality of his crop what he could not supply in quantity. The small Tidewater farm, as a rule, produced the best tobacco because a freeman cared more about his crop than a slave did about his master's. But perhaps this freeman had worked so hard that he, too, was now the owner of many acres and many slaves. Or perhaps he had moved and was now established farther inland or farther north, starting the struggle all over.

Perhaps industry and ambition were not strong in him. Instead, he liked the free and easy, semi-Indian life of the frontier. In that case, he might have moved still farther away from Tidewater—built himself a log cabin in the foothills of the Blue Ridge maybe and lived in the woods, mainly by hunting and trapping, trading with the Indians, fishing the upper waters of the great rivers. When civilization threatened to come close to him, he would move again, to the next river valley. Unwittingly he was the spearhead of settlement, of the ordered life he hated.

The price of tobacco on the London market would be of little concern to such a man. But to the others, the price of tobacco was all-important, and when it stabilized after 1690 at about 2*d* a pound, they prospered.

Smuggling

Slavery contributed to this prosperity by making it possible to produce the crop cheaply in large quantities. Another important factor, which served to spread the benefits around, was smuggling.

Smuggling was rampant in England from the days of the Commonwealth to the Napoleonic Wars. Whole districts were engaged "on the trade." Gentlemen, even the clergy, did not scruple to buy the smuggler's wares, and to the workingman the smuggler was a hero, who brought him his pleasures—his brandy, his tea, his tobacco—at prices he could pay.

Englishmen, Scots, Dutchmen, New Englanders all "ran" tobacco—both out of Virginia and into England. Even while the legitimate tobacco fleet was gathering in Chesapeake Bay, small, fast vessels were visiting back creeks and inlets, buying whatever any planter would sell. Usually this meant inferior grades of tobacco or leaf adulterated with stalks and ground leaves, but sometimes the very best tobacco was reserved for the smugglers' fleet. The smuggler could afford to pay the planter more for it and still undersell his legitimate rival in England or on the Continent, because he evaded the customs duty. Many bought cargoes openly at the central receiving warehouses and departed lightheartedly for some secret cove in Britain.

The most strenuous efforts of the Navy, of the customs men, of troops could not do more than put a dent in this vast traffic. Smugglers soon became hardened professionals, knowing every trick of the trade. Fore-and-aft rigging, which enabled a crew to maneuver a sailing vessel with much greater dexterity and speed than square rigging, was probably invented by the Dutch just for the business of smuggling; Yankee shipbuilders were quick to imitate them, and soon slim schooners were slipping down the New England ways and off to the Chesapeake to buy tobacco to run. And it was this tremendous flouting of the excise laws that enabled the poor European to smoke "Virginia" and the poor Virginian to keep his farm in competition with his slave-owning neighbor.

And yet, despite the great loss of income entailed by all this smuggling —not to mention the almost universal cheating on the part of English merchants—the profits to the Crown from tobacco duty were the envy of Europe. This one product alone brought in four times the revenue of Britain's entire trade with the Far East. From 1619 until 1685, every colonial governor arrived with instructions from the king to discourage Virginians from relying exclusively on this one crop. But from Effingham on, nothing more was heard about diversification. In the eyes of

James Blair, ecclesiastical deputy for Virginia, sponsored and pleaded for the founding of a college in the colony.

the government, Virginia existed to produce customs duty and consume English goods.

In 1693, when requested to draw up a charter and provide funds for a college to be established in the colony, Comptroller Sir Edward Seymour objected. A waste of money—what did a lot of crude colonials want with a college?

James Blair, Virginia's ecclesiastical deputy whose pet project the college was, pleaded that the new foundation would produce much-needed ministers of the Gospel. "The people of Virginia have souls to be saved as well as the people of England," he said.

"Souls!" cried Sir Edward, astounded at such effrontery. "Damn your souls! Make tobacco!"

The College

The Reverend Mr. Blair obtained his charter nonetheless, because King William and Queen Mary favored the idea and because he himself was a person of overwhelming character and determination, destined to be a power in the colony—a maker and breaker of governors—for half a century.

He had come to Virginia in 1685, an ordained minister, and five years later the Bishop of London, in whose diocese Virginia was included, appointed Blair his commissary, or deputy, for the colony. In 1689, when the Assembly began to discuss the possibility of establishing a college in Virginia, Blair embraced the scheme with enthusiasm. The colonists subscribed £2,000 for the endowment, and Colonel John Page gave part of his estate at Middle Plantation as a site. Then the Assembly drew up a petition to the monarchs, requesting a charter, and sent Blair to London to deliver it.

The king and queen were graciously pleased to grant the charter and to appoint Blair president of the new foundation. Spurred by his success, the commissary diligently sought and obtained additional donations throughout England. In 1695, after his return to Virginia, construction was begun on a building believed to have been designed by Sir Christo-

The central building at William and Mary is thought to have been built from a design by Sir Christopher Wren.

pher Wren. Three years later it opened its doors as the College of William and Mary.

Meanwhile, Blair had embroiled himself in politics. He had returned from England to find Francis Nicholson replaced by Sir Edmund Andros, a stormy petrel who had already got into trouble trying to govern New York and later had so enraged Massachusetts settlers that they had imprisoned him and shipped him back to England. He and Blair quarreled almost as soon as the latter disembarked. Andros feared that Blair's efforts to reform the church in Virginia would divert revenue from the colony's treasury to that of the church. Blair saw Sir Edmund as an obstacle to the completion of his beloved college. He used his influence in England to have Andros recalled.

Nicholson returned as governor just in time for the second Jamestown fire, an event that took place on October 31, 1698. The capital had been rebuilt after Bacon's destruction, but it had never proved a popular place to live, and now men began to talk of shifting the seat of government to a more healthful site. Why not Middle Plantation, near the new college?

There was nothing in the area but the Wren Building, Bruton Parish Church, and the remains of the old cross-peninsula palisade against the Indians. But it had good springs of water, and its location made it equally accessible to all parts of the York-James peninsula. When the Assembly met the following April, it was in the Wren Building. There, Governor Nicholson told the House of Burgesses:

"I do now cordially recomend to you the Placing of your publick Building (which God willing you are designed to have) somewhere at Middle Plantation nigh his Majesties Royall Colledg of William and Mary."

The General Assembly agreed. Virginia was doing well for herself, for the king, for the empire. It was time she had a proper capital.

A spacious little town was accordingly laid out and building begun. Queen Mary was dead by then, so they named it for the king: Williamsburg.

CHAPTER SIX

Without Limits to Our Bounds

Governor Nicholson took a lead in planning Williamsburg. A street almost a mile long was laid out eastward from the Wren Building to the site of the new government building, which was to be called the Capitol. This principal avenue was named Duke of Gloucester Street after the son of Princess Anne, heiress to the throne. Two parallel streets bore the names of the governor—Francis Street on the south and Nicholson Street on the north. In order that the town should not be crowded or carelessly laid out, strict building regulations were established: Lots had to be at least half an acre each, and houses on the

Spacious and attractive, Williamsburg was the beautiful capital of a sprawling colony.

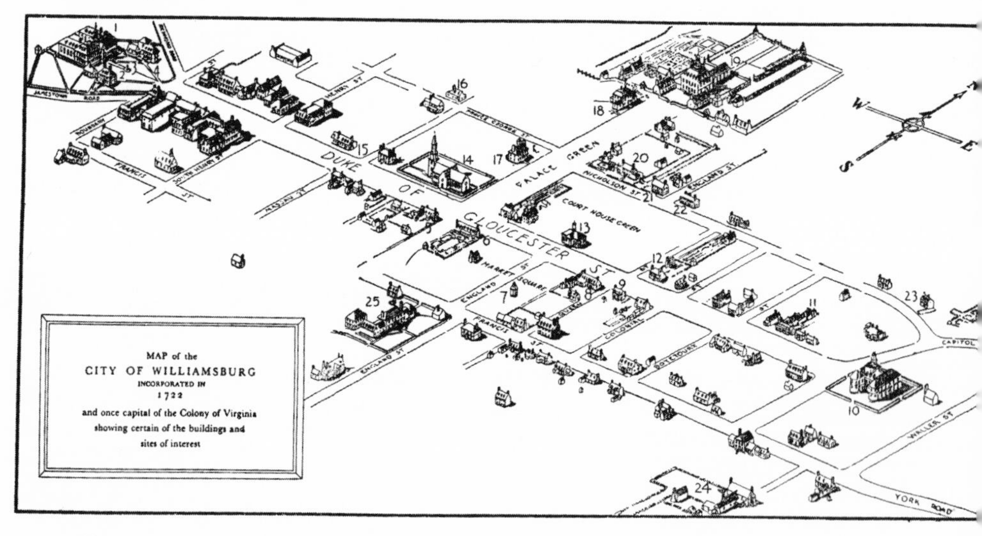

The Capitol, where the House of Burgesses sat, was the scene of much famous oratory and landmark legislation.

main streets could not be smaller than a certain minimum size or built within a certain distance of the roadway.

New architectural fashions were imported from England for both "publick Building" and private—great hipped roofs, broken by dormers, tall, slender chimneys, clock towers and cupolas, Palladian windows. Houses were being erected, wrote historian Robert Beverley, with "their Stories much higher than formerly, and their Windows large, and Sasht with Cristal Glass." Most of these were clapboard; but where brick was employed, it was laid in handsomely patterned Flemish bond—bricks laid alternately lengthwise and endwise. Plans were made for a governor's mansion to stand halfway between the Wren Building and the Capitol, surrounded by spacious and carefully landscaped grounds, and many plantation owners built themselves residences for use in "Publick Times."

For eighty years this little town was to be the center of culture, trade, and politics for a great colony which at one time was spread as far west as the Mississippi and as far north as the borders of Quebec.

The Governor's Palace took fourteen years to build, but when complete, it was the handsomest building in the colonies.

Here, Anne was proclaimed queen in 1702. Here, in later years, the three Georges were proclaimed king. Here, some of the greatest of America's founding fathers were to have their training in law and leadership.

Alexander Spotswood

Ironically, the little prince for whom the town's chief thoroughfare had been named died of scarlet fever two years before his mother ascended the throne. Ironically, too, the man who had given his name to two other streets did not last much longer.

Francis Nicholson quarreled as violently with James Blair as Andros had—perhaps more violently, for the middle-aged governor had a savage temper and was peculiarly unbalanced during the period by having fallen in love with a slip of a girl who did not return his love. The upshot was that Blair managed to get him recalled in 1704. Three short-term interim governors followed. Then in 1710 Virginia had the good fortune to come under the governorship of Alexander Spotswood.

Spotswood was a Scot from a military and clerical family. His great-great-grandfather, as Archbishop of St. Andrews, had crowned Scotland's King James VI (later James I of England). The son of an army surgeon, Alexander himself had entered the army at the age of seventeen as an ensign in the Earl of Bath's regiment of foot. In ten years he advanced to the rank of lieutenant colonel, when he was appointed to Marlborough's staff as assistant quartermaster general. He was wounded at Blenheim and captured at Oudenaarde; then, with Queen Anne's War dwindling to a close, he received his appointment to Virginia. He was thirty-four.

Like Nicholson, Spotswood was officially lieutenant governor. The Crown had discovered that it could increase the number of appointive offices at its disposal—and thus the number of votes it could influence in Parliament—by bestowing the official title and half the salary on a peer or other political bigwig, while naming a professional subordinate to do the actual work.

Spotswood was particularly welcome to Virginians, for he brought them the right to habeas corpus. In turn, he was pleased with them. "I have a fair prospect of a good Agreement with the People," he wrote soon after his arrival, "& believe I shall live very contentedly here." Imaginative and energetic, he immediately stamped the new little capital with the imprint of his personality.

He added the Palace Green to the town plan. When it was decided to rebuild old Bruton Parish Church to suit the new styles, Governor Spotswood was asked to design it, which he did with great success. He also designed the curious little octagonal powder magazine with a roof as tall as its walls, enlarged the town jail, helped with the layout and design of the governor's mansion—Governor's Palace, they had begun to call it—and pressed to see that it was completed. "This is a Matter in which Your Own Honour is . . . engaged," he reminded the Council, in urging them to supply the necessary funds. Because the money was so slow in forthcoming, it took fourteen years to complete the Palace.

When the job was done, however, Williamsburg had what was probably the handsomest building of its kind in North America. Hugh Jones, an English professor of mathematics at the college, described it in glowing terms:

"A magnificent structure, built at the publick expense, finished and beautified with gates, fine gardens, offices, walks, a fine canal, orchards, etc. with a great number of the best arms nicely posited by the ingenious contrivance of the most accomplished Colonel Spotswood."

Blackbeard

An "ingenious contrivance" of the governor in another field was his campaign against the pirates who infested American waters. In 1700 Governor Nicholson had personally led an expedition against a pirate ship that had entered Chesapeake Bay and captured several merchant ships; after a ten-hour battle, during which the collector of customs for Virginia, who had accompanied Nicholson, was killed at the governor's side, the pirate ship was captured and about sixty men taken prisoner.

During Queen Anne's War, most pirates were able to obtain letters of marque, enabling them to prey on French commerce as legitimate

Lieutenant Maynard sails home in triumph with the head of Blackbeard lashed to his bowsprit and fifteen prisoners.

privateers. But at war's end, in 1713, they went back to plain piracy. In 1717 Governor Spotswood complained:

"Our Capes have been for these six Weeks pass'd in a manner blocked up by those pyrates, and diverse Ships inward bound, taken and plundered by them."

A man-of-war was stationed along the Virginia capes in an attempt to guard shipping, but it was in such unseaworthy condition that it was unable to attack the well-armed pirates. Two more king's ships were dispatched from England at Spotswood's urgent request, and they succeeded to some extent in controlling piracy in Chesapeake Bay. But Virginia shipping was still at the mercy of a "nest of pyrates" who took refuge in North Carolina. Hiding among the inlets and shallow-water bays of Pamlico Sound, these men would dart out without warning, swarm all over their prey, then dash back to their refuges where the deep-keeled ships could not follow.

The most notorious of these was Edward Teach, known as Blackbeard from his habit of flaunting his long beard by wearing it in sausage curls or pigtails tied with ribbon. Teach had good connections in North Carolina. The secretary of the governor allowed his barn to be used by the pirate as a warehouse, and Governor Charles Eden himself was said to have received a bribe of sixty barrels of sugar to look the other way. Teach made his headquarters in the Pamlico River, where he and twenty or thirty followers lived in wild debauchery, raiding as they pleased, demanding tribute from ships passing up the river, and forcing neighboring planters to supply them with food and drink. These planters, realizing that they could expect no help from their own governor, appealed to Virginia. Spotswood acted promptly.

Because so many people, including Virginians, had "an unaccountable inclination to favor pyrates," Spotswood planned his expedition with great secrecy. With his own money he hired two sloops, then sent to the frigates *Pearl* and *Lyme* for officers and crew to man them. Unlike Nicholson, Spotswood did not join the group in person, perhaps feeling that sea fighting was best left to professionals. Robert Maynard, first lieutenant of the *Pearl*, was put in command.

Lieutenant Maynard's two sloops left Hampton on November 17, 1718, and five days later came upon Blackbeard's ship *Adventure* in Okracoke Inlet, not far from Cape Hatteras. Maynard's vessels carried no cannon, but the pirate ship did, and Blackbeard opened a murderous fire as soon as the sloops came into range, his guns loaded to the muzzle with swan shot.

One sloop was disabled, but Maynard sent everyone below but himself and the helmsman and managed to put his vessel alongside the *Adventure*. Blackbeard and fourteen followers swarmed aboard the sloop, hoping to overpower it before the men could get back on deck. A ferocious hand-to-hand encounter ensued, "till the Sea was tinctur'd with Blood round the Vessel." Maynard and Blackbeard fought face to face until the pirate fell dead, pierced by twenty sword wounds and five pistol shots.

Meanwhile, the men of the second sloop got their vessel under control and boarded the *Adventure*. Another desperate and savage battle took place, but the Navy men had the advantage of numbers, and after another nine of the pirates had been killed, Blackbeard's men were subdued. Casualties among the king's men were high, too—ten killed and twenty-four wounded.

Maynard cut off Blackbeard's head and lashed it to his bowsprit, ribbons, beard, and all. Then, with fifteen prisoners in his hold, he sailed for Virginia, where the pirates were duly tried and hanged.

This episode made Spotswood so hated among what pirates were left that he wrote his government he dared not sail for England in anything but a king's ship.

Journey Through the Mountains

Alexander Spotswood was a man who could think in terms of empire. He advised the home government to do something about Spanish Florida, which sheltered and encouraged pirates who preyed on all British shipping. When Indians threatened to overrun South Carolina, he sent arms and ammunition and later troops to aid Virginia's troubled neighbor—

Governor Alexander Spotswood, a vigorous and far-sighted executive, left a strong mark on Virginia.

an almost unheard-of example of cooperation between normally squabbling colonies. He pacified Virginia's own Indians, sided with them against the depredations of the lawless frontiersmen, tried to reorganize and control the Indian trade—although he failed in this because too many important Virginians were making too much money by means of it—and improved the Indian school at William and Mary. He tried to break the power of the great planters, who through their alliances with rich London merchants could bring pressure on the home government for grants of land and other special privileges. And he succeeded in establishing peace between Virginia and her neighbor to the south.

Bad blood had sprung up between Virginians, particularly Indian traders, and North Carolinians. North Carolina was notorious for the sanctuary it offered runaway servants and criminals from Virginia, and in turn she complained that Virginians were rustling North Carolina cattle. All this was aggravated by the fact that the exact placing of the boundary was uncertain. A strip of no-man's-land fifteen miles wide lay in dispute.

Spotswood set himself to clearing up this confusion, and after five

Half for political reasons, half for pure frolic, Spotswood leads an expedition across the Blue Ridge.

years of negotiation with Carolina officials, he at last reached an agreement with Governor Eden. The boundary line was not settled for good until after Spotswood had retired, but its course was based on the understanding between the two governors.

Perhaps the governor's most important characteristic was his ability to see that the future of Englishmen in the New World lay toward the west and that it was time men's eyes were turned in that direction.

From her first charter, Virginia had laid claim to all the land to the westward as far as the Great South Sea (the Pacific Ocean—named South Sea by the Spanish, who first came upon it by crossing the Isthmus of Panama from north to south). "We are bounded to the Eastward by the Virginian Sea," wrote Governor Nicholson in 1699, "to the Westward at present without Limits to our Bounds." Settlement had already pushed out of Tidewater into the geographical region known as the Piedmont, an area of rolling hills that lay between the falls of the rivers and the Blue Ridge. Beyond those distant mountains, however, few Englishmen had yet ventured. Governor Spotswood wanted to be one of them.

The expedition he planned was to be partly a pleasure excursion, partly a way of seeing what lay beyond the mountains, and partly a political expedient on behalf of his master, King George I. For it had not escaped Governor Spotswood's notice that France, not content with Quebec and some trading posts on the Great Lakes, had established a settlement at the mouth of the Mississippi and named it after Louis XIV. If Quebec were to establish a firm link with Louisiana, the French would control the Mississippi and effectively block all western expansion. Spotswood wanted to firm up British claims to the continent.

So in August, 1716, he set off for "A Mont[h]s Expedition w'th 63 Men & 74 Horses," over the crest of the Blue Ridge.

Excursion

Whatever its political implications, the trip was an exciting, carefree excursion through the woods. Among the many gentlemen who went were Robert Beverley, an early historian of the colony, and John Fontaine, a Huguenot émigré, who kept a diary of the expedition. In addition they were accompanied by Negro servants, four Meherrin Indians, and fourteen frontier-bred scouts. They hunted deer and bear, fished, and admired the magnificent scenery of a region still famed for its beauty.

They found the source of the Rappahannock, where that river "runs no bigger than a man's arm, from under a large stone." When they reached the summit of the Blue Ridge at Swift Run Gap, they stopped to drink the health of King George and as many of the royal family as they could remember. They had plenty of liquids to drink it in: red and white wine of Virginia, Irish whiskey, brandy, shrub (a fruit-and-alcohol mixture), rum, champagne, canary, punch, cider, and so on.

When they entered the broad Shenandoah Valley, they claimed the land in the king's name. They again celebrated. Wrote Fontaine:

"We had a good dinner, and after it we got the men together, and loaded all their arms, and we drank the King's health in champagne, and fired a volly; and the Princess' health in burgundy, and fired a volly; and all the rest of the royal family in claret, and a volly."

Before heading up into the rough terrain of the Piedmont and the mountains, they had had to have their horses shod, a practice not always necessary in the sandy soil of Tidewater. Upon their return to Williamsburg, Governor Spotswood presented each of his companions with a golden horseshoe as a memento of the expedition. On one side it carried an inscription: *Sic juvat transcendere montes*, "In this fashion, it is pleasant to cross the mountains."

More About Diversification

In the wake of this expedition and Spotswood's announcement that he himself planned to make his home permanently in Virginia, two new counties were created, Brunswick in the southern part of the colony, and Spotsylvania—named for the popular governor—in the northern. In 1728, on a large tract of land in the latter county, the governor settled with a new wife and lived out his life as postmaster general for the colonies.

Conflicts with Blair and with the powerful planters on the Council had caused him to be removed from the governorship in 1722, but his popularity in the colony remained strong. He had begun to identify with her interests rather than those of the home government. The Crown might be happy with its tobacco revenues and ask no more of Virginia than that she grow her staple crop. But Spotswood could see that this was economically dangerous for Virginia herself and tried to stimulate production of hemp, tar, timber, and other naval stores. He himself set an example by importing a group of German ironworkers and establishing them near his new home, to mine ore and set up a furnace to smelt it.

But few Virginians heeded him. They were doing all right for themselves with tobacco, thank you. For the snuff craze had hit England.

CHAPTER SEVEN

Just Arrived, the Success's Increase

Snuff was tobacco ground to a very fine powder and inhaled. Snuffing had been fashionable in France, Italy, and Spain for decades before it caught the fancy of Englishmen. It was a foible particularly associated with Roman Catholic clerics, and popes twice had to issue official rebukes to those priests who indulged while actually engaged in saying Mass. (In 1755 Benedict XIV revoked earlier bans on snuffing; Benedict was a snuffer himself.)

French snuff makers first ground and sifted the leaf (preferably "Spanish") to a very fine dust, then colored it with various dyes and perfumed it with bergamot, verbena, attar of roses, or any fragrance desired. A fashionable *débitant de tabac* offered dozens of varieties to choose from.

The snuff taker caught up a pinch of *tabac râpé* from his *tabatière*—a container encrusted with enamel and gold and jewels if he was rich—spread the powder out on the back of his hand, and sniffed first with one nostril and then the other. Then, *achoo!* Not only was the sneeze itself pleasurable, but afterward there remained much the same narcotic sense of well-being that smoking gave.

The snuff habit took England by storm in a curious way. In 1702 in one of the early engagements of Queen Anne's War, the British and Dutch fleets attacked and captured a Spanish treasure fleet in Vigo Bay. In the excitement over this success, no one paid much attention to another group of prizes, taken off Puerta de Santa Maria about the same time: tobacco ships laden with the finest Spanish snuff. These prizes

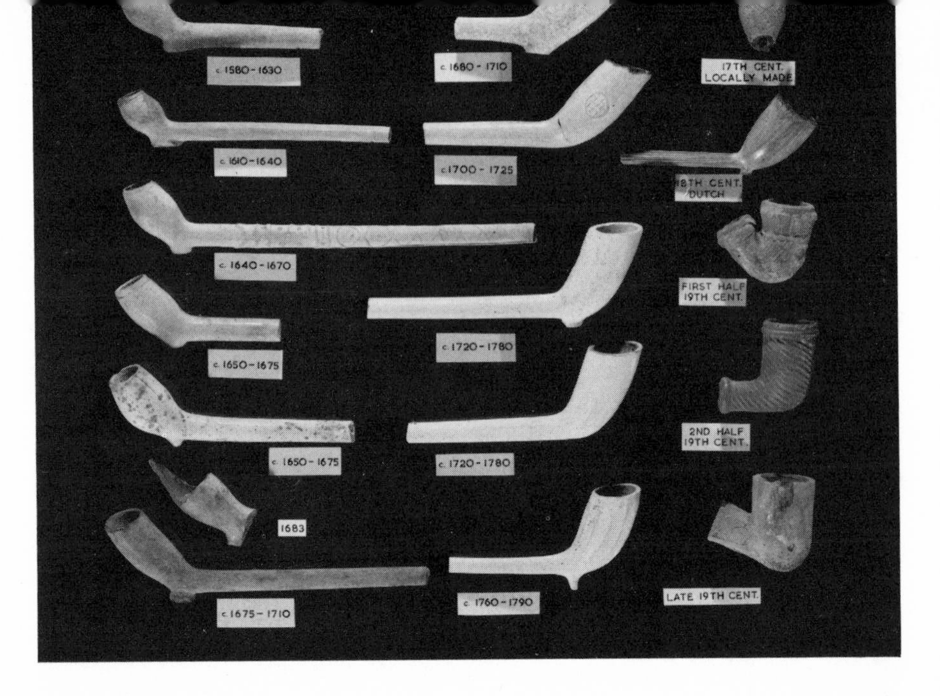

Clay tobacco pipes excavated at Colonial Williamsburg. Much of the yard-long stem is missing from some.

were unloaded in the Channel ports and their cargoes sold cheap. Poor commoners found themselves in possession of snuff intended for French aristocrats. Overnight the habit spread all over England and to Scotland and Ireland.

At first the rich snubbed this common man's pleasure. Then Queen Anne's courtiers began to try it, and soon snuffing was as fashionable in England as it had been on the Continent.

Many men still smoked, of course, although the short clay pipe of the seventeenth century was slowly giving way to the long-stemmed "yard of clay" of the eighteenth. But now that snuffing was here, women (who had not followed the example of Queen Elizabeth's pipe-smoking ladies-in-waiting) took up the use of tobacco, greatly widening the market. An elaborate etiquette sprang up, with strict rules as to just how, when, and under what circumstances one used which form of snuff, to whom and with what gestures one offered one's snuffbox for a polite exchange. A new art form developed as artisans vied in creating beautiful or ingeniously shaped snuffboxes, and there were rules about giving these as gifts, too.

Once that first windfall of "Spanish" was gone, common people fell back on Sweet Scented, which they used plain, grinding their own leaf in a special little wooden mortar and pestle called a mull. For the rich a new trade sprang up: snuff maker. The leaf was ground in horse-operated machines and carefully graded. The English preferred their snuff less dyed and perfumed than the French did, but they were particular about its quality nonetheless.

Plantation Life, Mid-Eighteenth Century

With the snuff habit to increase the demand for tobacco and slavery to make its production cheaper, Virginia planters prospered. They showed it in the grand new estates they began to erect along the rivers: Little England, 1716, Rosewell, 1721, Shirley, 1769, Hedgelawn, 1723, Montpelier, 1760, Berkeley, 1726, Stratford Hall, 1729, Westover, 1730,

Carter's Grove, one of numerous eighteenth-century plantation houses that still grace Virginian scenery.

Kingston Hall, 1730, Warner Hall, 1740, White Marsh, 1750, Poplar Grove, 1750, Hopemount, 1750, Carter's Grove, 1751, Wilton, 1753, Gunston Hall, 1755, and many others whose precise dates are unknown —Brandon, River Edge, Belleville, Corotoman, Tar Bay House, Eastover, Claremont Manor, Nomini Hall, Goshen, Exchange, Toddsbury.

The old-fashioned hall-and-parlor house was given up or made into a dower house or turned over to the overseer. Perhaps, as often happened, it accidentally burned down, and the owner used this occasion as an excuse to rebuild in the grand manner. For a plantation could no longer be a mere haphazard collection of buildings. It had to be laid out in formal style, preferably symmetrical, and be surrounded by walls, ornamental ironwork gates with heraldic figures on them, gardens of box and espaliered fruit trees and flowers, lawns, tree-lined drives.

The house itself, though it was seldom enormous like the English country houses of the period, had to look a bit imposing and provide plenty of room for spacious and airy chambers and numerous bedrooms to accommodate visitors. The house was usually flanked by outbuildings that matched the main building in style but were smaller in ground plan and height. One of these would probably be the schoolhouse, where the planter's children were taught their letters, probably by some impoverished Scots dominie brought over on indentures. The other might be a detached ballroom or library, the planter's private study or the plantation office, where books were kept on all the many transactions in which the owner might be engaged. On the second floor of these flanking buildings there would probably be yet more bedrooms, for visiting had become an important occupation in the planter's life of increasing leisure.

Farther from the house, preferably hidden by some tactfully planted shrubbery, would be the more workaday structures: the kitchen (always a separate building because of the heat), the laundry, the stables, the coach house, the smithy, the cooperage, the dairy, the carpentry shop, the tannery, the shoemaker's workroom, the weaving-and-spinning house, the distillery, the smokehouse, the icehouse, the kitchen garden, and, of course, the slave quarters.

Tobacco built all this, but a tobacco house would not be part of the home farm; tobacco houses were built out in the fields near the growing crop. Somewhere nearby—but probably also hidden from the house—was the tobacco warehouse where the packed hogsheads awaited shipment, and possibly a wharf as well, for most planters received cargo right at their doors.

Who operated all these enterprises? Slaves, largely. By 1740, blacks outnumbered whites in Virginia. Some planters would import artisans from England or Europe purely to teach slaves their crafts. Once learned, a craft became one more thing by which the planter could profit, because he might rent out his slave's services to a neighbor.

Most slaves were well treated, but it was the good treatment of a man to his livestock. Slaves represented a large investment to their owner, and it only made sense to see that they were fed and clothed adequately, given a holiday now and then, not left to the wasteful mistreatment of a brutal overseer. Wrote Robert Beverley, "Slaves are not worked near so hard, nor so many Hours a Day, as the Husbandmen, and Day-Labourers in England." But they were "worked."

A large plantation was a complicated little world of its own and one that took a lot of management. A planter had to be an able administrator, a shrewd merchant, a knowledgeable farmer rolled into one. Most of all, he had to master the difficult art of governing people. The habit of ruling came naturally to plantation society—so naturally that four out of the first five American presidents were Virginians. But often the home plantation was only the headquarters of what was by now a private empire—tens of thousands, occasionally hundreds of thousands, of acres.

Land, Land, Land

By 1740 the rich planter was very rich indeed and immensely powerful. He used his wealth and position to acquire more land and yet more, and sometimes he did not scruple to cheat to do so. He could get away with it because he was serving as sheriff or judge or member of the governor's council or burgess or as an officer in the militia, and was related by blood or marriage to most other magnates as well.

Some of these land grants were enormous—twenty thousand acres, forty thousand, a hundred thousand. In 1749 the Ohio Company, an alliance of rich planters and London merchants, was granted 500,000 acres in the Ohio Valley by the Privy Council itself, and the colony, at about the same time, gave away a lavish 800,000 acres of border land to yet another private group. There were, of course, millions of acres to grant.

Many smallholders still held out, living much as their grandfathers had lived in the seventeenth century, surviving by growing a quality crop, owning a slave or two, sending their sons to William and Mary. But the Tidewater was dominated by the great landholders, who kept the important offices in their own hands. Able to afford private education for their own children, they refused to vote public funds for free state schools, so many Virginians grew up illiterate.

The rich planter did not need as much land as he owned and often made no attempt to settle or clear his acres, so that great stretches of the countryside remained woods and marshland. A planter wanted vast holdings partly for speculation—to sell off later at a good price or to settle his sons on—and partly for grandeur. In England, to own a large landed estate meant to be a gentleman, and the eighteenth-century Virginia planter was determined above everything to be an English gentleman.

So he bought English furniture and silver, hand-painted Chinese wallpaper, a coach with his armorial bearings on the door, silks and laces for his wife and daughters, velvets and broadcloths for himself, books and paintings and musical instruments, crystal chandeliers, elaborately framed mirrors, blooded horses, all the delights of gracious living. If he could bring himself to risk the smallpox and plague that were so common in the Old World, he might send his children to be educated entirely in England. Or he might content himself with dispatching his teen-age son to Oxford and for the Grand Tour of the Continent that was considered essential to finish off a young man's education.

An eighteenth-century parlor. Sophisticated and elegant Virginians could well afford to cultivate graceful living.

But often he preferred to educate his children at home, to train them in the elaborate manners that were becoming the hallmark of rich Virginians, who prided themselves on their courtliness.

The Pleasures of Life

Hospitality was a way of life with these people. Living at such distances from one another, the great planters could only see new faces, enjoy a bit of gaming, exchange gossip of London by visiting their friends. Usually a man got out the coach and perhaps a cart or two for the baggage, and took the whole family. A visit was expected to last—a week, two weeks, a month, sometimes half a year. Perhaps when one family had concluded its visit to another, the second would return to be guests of the first. They were probably kin in some degree anyway.

But one did not have to rely on relatives for accommodation. Traveling strangers were always welcomed with enthusiasm and bounty. Observed Robert Beverley:

"The Inhabitants are very courteous to Travellers. . . . A Stranger has no more to do, but to inquire upon the Road, where any Gentleman, or good House-keeper lives, and there he may depend upon being received with Hospitality."

Visitors to Virginia observed that one could travel through the entire colony with no money except what was needed to pay for ferry crossings, and that consequently there were very few inns or ordinaries for public accommodation.

In the company of his friends, the Virginia planter enjoyed horse racing, hunting, cockfighting. Balls and concerts were frequent. In 1716 the first theater in the English colonies was erected in Williamsburg, where "Comedies, Drolls, or other kind of stage plays" were acted.

The high point of the planter's year—higher even perhaps than the day the tobacco fleet was sighted, bringing all the lovely things he had ordered from his broker—was the Publick Times. This was the time, twice a year, when the rate of exchange was established, bills were bought and sold, and the meeting of the general court held. The planter would have his horse saddled and with his body servant riding behind him—and perhaps a groom as well, for show—he would set off for the capital to take his part in the colony's affairs.

Interior of Christ Church, in the little town of Alexandria. The Anglican Church was established in Virginia.

Town Life

Although Williamsburg never acquired a large permanent population or achieved the status of city, it saw plenty of bustle in its heyday. One foreign visitor complained of the Virginians' rowdiness:

"In the Day Time People hurying back and forwards from the Capitoll to the Taverns, and at Night carousing and drinking in one Chamber and Box and Dice in another, which continues till Morning commonly."

Williamsburg was not the only town in Virginia. Many little seaports had sprung up to service the tobacco fleet: Norfolk, Hampton, Yorktown, Newport News. In addition, by mid-eighteenth century, Virginia could boast of several thriving inland towns, situated mostly at the falls of the rivers: Alexandria on the Potomac, Falmouth and Fredericksburg on the Rappahannock, Richmond on the James, Petersburg on the Appomattox. Towns were useful for supplying specialty trades. Not even the wealthiest planter kept his own wigmaker, his own glazier, his own apothecary. Most towns could boast of saddlers, shoemakers, harnessmakers, silversmiths, tanners, gunsmiths, tailors, cabinetmakers. Towns fostered a middle class and gave the freed bondman a place to set up for himself.

New Kinds of Immigration

The big planters controlled Tidewater, but they did not control Virginia–not quite. The back country had begun to fill up with new settlers of new sorts, and as new counties were formed, the House of Burgesses had to be enlarged to make room for their representatives. These newcomers were nearly all smallholders, and they brought a new element into Virginia politics.

Some were overflows from Pennsylvania. Drawn to the New World by William Penn's offer of religious tolerance, many Germans–often, but by no means always, members of small, persecuted sects–had poured into Philadelphia and west to the Susquehanna region. As those lands filled up, the flow turned south through the Shenandoah Valley, which lay between the Blue Ridge and the Allegheny Mountains.

German settlers introduced a building that was to have very nearly as much influence on American culture as the log cabin: the bank barn. This large building—often a hundred feet long and forty feet high—was the forerunner of nearly all dairy and general-purpose barns in use today. It was built on three levels. Cattle and horse stalls occupied the ground level, a threshing floor and general storeroom the middle level, with a loft above for hay. The distinguishing feature of the structure was the bank, or wagon ramp, which permitted hay wains to be driven right into the middle level. If topography allowed it, the barn was built on a hillside to take advantage of the natural slope.

The Germans were general farmers and did not go into large-scale tobacco raising. Instead, they turned the broad Shenandoah Valley into a garden—flourishing orchards, lush fields of wheat and corn, smiling pastureland. Where they settled they stayed, and their children after them. Later generations of German immigrants scattered and were absorbed quickly into the general population. But these early comers formed tight-knit stable communities of their own, retaining their own language, art forms, and culture patterns well into the twentieth century.

More restless and turbulent were the Scotch-Irish immigrants who flowed in at about the same time. These were Presbyterian Scots from the north of Ireland, where their families had been deliberately planted about the time Virginia herself was first settled. High rents and English restrictions on Irish commerce had impoverished them and driven many to emigrate. Many others came directly from Scotland, traders or teachers. (Literacy had a broader base in Scotland than in England, so there were plenty of poor dominies to be exported.) So many Scots emigrated to the colonies, in fact, that one battle of the Revolution, King's Mountain, was fought almost wholly by Scots on both sides.

There were strong ties between Virginia and Scotland. Prior to the Act of Union, 1707, the Scots had been excluded from trade with the colonies, like any foreign country. So they took to smuggling. They were so successful at this that, after trade was legitimized, many Scots went into the tobacco-importing business legally; and by the time of the Revolution, Glasgow outranked London and all other ports as a tobacco center.

A tough, fiercely independent people, the Scots took naturally to life on the Virginia frontier. They fanned out into the mountain valleys, then on south into North Carolina. A family would settle, build itself a cabin and live a few years, then up stakes and move on. Some of the men became "long hunters," vanishing into the wilderness for months at a time, probing the mysterious lands beyond the Alleghenies—the Ohio Valley, the Illinois country, the fertile no-man's-land the Indians called Kentucky.

These newcomers opened up the country's first "West" and began to provide a counterbalance to the plantation society of Tidewater. So many poured in during the 1740's that the racial balance shifted once more, and Negroes were again outnumbered. These new Virginians demanded representation in the House of Burgesses and began to press upon the burgesses the needs of the common man. They had cut their ties with Europe and were little impressed with claims upon their loyalty by a distant king and a government beyond the ocean. Little heed was paid to their complaints as yet, but their day was to come.

Bond Servant and Slave

White indentured labor was still a source of immigrants. Bond servants were usually sea captains' ventures—part of the cargo that was carried over in the ship that would return crammed with tobacco. A laboring man would sign an indenture with a ship's master for his passage. When the ship arrived at Yorktown or Norfolk or Hampton, the captain would advertise in the newspaper the date of his sale:

"Just arrived, the *Success's Increase*, Captain Curtis, with about eighty choice healthy Servants, among whom are many Tradesmen, viz. Shoemakers, Weavers, Carpenters, Black [iron] and White [tin] Smiths, Tailors, a Sailmaker. . . ."

Slaves attend market, each with a small basket of things to sell. Perhaps they are earning their freedom.

If all the servants were not sold within a reasonable time, the rest would be sold to a "soul-driver" who would "drive them through the country" until he had sold off all their indentures for a profit. If all else failed, soul-drivers could always peddle their wares in the Shenandoah Valley, where labor was chronically in short supply.

Black slaves, too, were sold off the vessel that had brought them and often ended up in the possession of soul-drivers. It is estimated that twenty thousand Negroes a year were imported into the American colonies, chiefly the southern ones. These were the survivors—seven out of eight taken aboard in the Bight of Benin—of the brutal Middle Passage, where sharks trailed the slavers across the Atlantic. In the so-called triangular trade, a slave trader left Liverpool or Rhode Island with a cargo of trade goods, sailed for the west coast of Africa, where he bargained with a local factor for the contents of his barracoon—a warehouse where slaves were kept until enough had been accumulated to form a cargo—then crossed the Atlantic as fast as possible (for the cargo was perishable) to the West Indies or the mainland colonies, where the slaves were sold for sugar or tobacco, then home.

The slave trade came into disrepute long before slavery itself did, primarily because slave owners had begun to be haunted by fear of an uprising. Some Virginians, as early as 1699, made an effort to control or diminish the importation of Negroes by placing a high import duty on the traffic. But this action was disallowed by the English government, acting on behalf of English merchants and slave traders. Still, even in a callous age, the act of buying and selling a human being was hard to witness, and as the eighteenth century began to make humanitarianism fashionable, the tide of public opinion in England itself slowly turned against the slavers.

Meanwhile, there was little a slave fresh from Africa could do about his plight—stranded in a strange land among people who spoke a strange tongue and drove him to till a strange new crop. Even if he could escape, how could he get home again? He didn't even know in which direction home lay, and as for operating the white man's ships, which seemed to move by magic without anyone to paddle, this was beyond his comprehension altogether. (Most slaves were taken from inland tribes, and many had never seen the sea before they arrived at the barracoon.) Many black men did struggle fiercely against enslavement, but troublemakers were often dumped overboard at sea or committed suicide by jumping, so that what arrived in Virginia was the subdued portion of the cargo. Most resigned themselves to their fate. Bewilderment made them docile.

If a slave did run off and was caught and brought back, he was liable to be whipped—although crueler punishments were employed with chronic runaways. A white bond servant, if he ran away or caused trouble in some other fashion, could be sued in the courts and have years of servitude added to his indentures. In return, he could sue his master if the latter failed to live up to the terms of their agreement and sometimes win a reduction in time or even his freedom.

It was possible, if conditions were exactly right, for a slave to buy himself free. He had to have a cooperative master, though—one who was not only willing to sell him at all but willing to arrange things so that earning the purchase price was possible. Some slave owners permitted their slaves to perform extra tasks for extra money—perhaps grow some vegetables on a little plot of their own behind the quarters. But all this had to be done on the slave's own time, after many hot hours in the tobacco fields.

Occasionally an African-born Negro did escape or buy himself free (although he seldom found his way back to Africa), but as a rule it wasn't until the second or third generation that a slave was sufficiently skilled or knowledgeable to free himself. If a free Negro had a trade to follow or managed to open a tavern or otherwise go into business for himself, he probably fared rather well. But if he had to hire out, he found that the most menial tasks were reserved for him—sweeping chimneys, emptying chamber pots, cleaning stables. On the other hand, an occasional free Negro thrived so well that he was able to buy slaves himself.

King George's War

King George's War came and went without much effect on Virginia. This confusing conflict started out in 1739 as a sea duel between England and Spain. Then in 1743 it swung about and became a European land war with England, Holland, and Austria on one side, and Prussia, France, Bavaria, and Spain on the other; the Jacobite Rising in 1745 in favor of Prince Charles Stuart served as a kind of sideshow to the main event. In 1743 at Dettingen on the Main, George II led his troops to a victory, the last time a British monarch was to do so in person. In 1748 the treaty of Aix-la-Chapelle was signed, bringing a shaky peace.

New England had been involved against France, and Georgia and the Carolinas against Spain. But Virginia, Maryland, and the Middle Colonies had had no vital interests at stake and had played the whole affair rather cool.

But the year after Aix-la-Chapelle, Virginia heard some news that hotted her up: The French were on the Ohio, laying claim to the region in the name of Louis XV.

CHAPTER EIGHT

His Enemies upon the Ohio

The news was brought by men who had been trading with the Indians of the Ohio Valley at Logstown (modern Ambridge, Pennsylvania) and Pickawillany (near modern Picqua, Ohio). On orders from the governor-general of Quebec, Captain Pierre-Joseph Céleron de Blainville had canoed across Lake Erie from Fort Niagara and portaged by way of Lake Chautauqua to the upper stretches of the Allegheny, which the French considered part of the Ohio proper. He had then proceeded down the Allegheny to its confluence with the Monongahela at the Forks and down the Ohio as far as the mouth of the Miami (near the modern Ohio-Indiana line). Here and there Céleron paused to bury lead plates, laying claim to the entire watershed of *la Belle Rivière*. Traders from both Pennsylvania and Virginia had warehouses and trading posts in the area. Céleron warned them all that the French had every intention of supporting their claims with force. Then he returned to Canada.

Nothing much happened immediately. Members of the Ohio Company, which included many of the most important families in Virginia, took alarm and sent Thomas Cresap, a Marylander, to blaze a trail through the mountains from the Potomac to the Forks, to make access to the region somewhat easier. Cresap hired a Delaware hunter named Nemacolin to show him the route used by Indians, and for a while the trail was called Nemacolin's Path. After that, trade went on with the Indians as usual.

But in the spring of 1752, the French sent an expedition of 240

Great Lakes Indians, led by two Frenchmen, against Pickawillany. They killed an Englishman and an old Miami chieftain and carried off seven Englishmen as prisoners to Canada, along with twenty thousand francs' worth of pelts. The following year, to make French intentions unmistakable, two thousand Canadians and French regulars arrived in what is now western Pennsylvania to establish forts at key positions along a new, shorter river route: Fort Presque Isle (near modern Erie), Fort Le Boeuf (modern Waterford) at the portage point between the lake and French Creek, and Fort Venango (modern Franklin) at the confluence of the creek with the Allegheny.

This news was too much for Robert Dinwiddie, Virginia's newly appointed governor. He had a personal interest in the region, being a member of the Ohio Company, but there were ample reasons of state for his indignation, too. In Virginia's view, the mountains formed Pennsylvania's western boundary; therefore, all the region beyond them to the Pacific was Virginia. The French had invaded the colony.

Dinwiddie sent a strong complaint to London and received instructions from George II's government: Warn them off. Accordingly, in

Twenty-one-year-old George Washington sets out for the Ohio carrying Governor Dinwiddie's letter.

the autumn of 1753, he looked about him for a suitable messenger. His choice was, to put it mildly, momentous.

Skirmishing

George Washington was young, only twenty-one, but he came of a good family, had been appointed adjutant of militia with the rank of major, and possessed an excellent acquaintance with the backcountry, having spent several years surveying in the mountain valleys. Moreover, he was a member of the Ohio Company, shares of which he had inherited from his older half-brother Lawrence, along with a 2,500-acre plantation on a bluff above the Potomac called Mount Vernon. In person he was tall and husky, complexion florid, hair reddish brown, eyes dark blue, face plain and rather pockmarked. He had not yet had a chance to exhibit his most outstanding characteristic: an almost total inability to panic.

To Major Washington, then, Governor Dinwiddie entrusted a letter to the French military commander, which warned him that he was on Virginia's soil and must leave. Young Washington left Williamsburg on October 31, 1753, picked up an interpreter and a guide, and vanished into the wilderness.

The following January 16, he reappeared in the capital with the answer of Captain Jacques Legardeur de St. Pierre, commandant at Fort Le Boeuf. Governor Dinwiddie's letter, said Legardeur courteously, had been forwarded to Governor-General Marquis Duquesne, to whom it should have been addressed in the first place; until further orders came from his superiors, he was obliged to remain where he was. In short, as Washington confirmed in a verbal report, the French were determined to hold the Ohio.

What to do now? The governor had already dispatched an advance party to start building some kind of fortification in the valley. But it was clear that troops were going to be needed. He issued a call for two hundred of Virginia's militia, then wrote to the governors of several other colonies for help. North Carolina was the only one to respond, offering a few hundred troops. Dinwiddie put these men under the official command of Joshua Fry, a colonel of the militia, promoted Washington to lieutenant colonel, made him second-in-command, and sent him to do what he could to support the fort builders. Then he turned to the problem of getting the London government to help.

Young Washington, the governor found, had brought back something else besides word of the French refusal to budge. He had kept a journal of his grueling winter journey, and it made exciting reading for men who had never glimpsed the vast American interior. Twice the governor's messenger had hairbreadth escapes from death—once from an Indian guide, who had suddenly turned enemy and fired at the major from pointblank range (he missed), once from falling into the ice-clogged Allegheny, nearly drowning, and having to spend a December night on a sandbar in the river.

Of the Forks, the surveyor-soldier wrote:

"I spent some Time in viewing the Rivers, and the Land in the Fork, which I think extremely well situated for a Fort, as it has absolute Command of both Rivers."

The governor recognized good propaganda material when he saw it. He had his own letter, Legardeur's reply, and Washington's journal printed up in pamphlet form, sent to England, and widely distributed. Overnight the name "George Washington" was known all over London, and officials who had yawned at the mention of the American colonies began to tell one another that it was time steps were taken.

First Clash

Washington spent the winter of 1754 frantically recruiting militia. He could not get the full 200 Virginians he was supposed to have, and his superior, Colonel Fry, did not bestir himself much to help. Finally, in the spring, Washington marched with 120 men to the support of the fort builders.

They weren't doing so well either. Directed to establish themselves at the Forks, they had managed to erect a modest stockade, which they called Fort Prince George after the king's grandson and heir, when a French flotilla appeared in the river: a thousand men, three hundred canoes, and eighteen cannon. The forty-one Virginians could only surrender. The French tut-tutted at their presence but turned them loose, and began to build their own somewhat larger fort, to be called Fort Duquesne. The dejected Virginia fort builders reached Washington at Wills Creek (modern Cumberland, Maryland) on April 22.

Obviously 161 Virginians couldn't take a fort from 1,000 Frenchmen with eighteen cannon. But they could establish an advance base and await reinforcements. Accordingly, they set out along Nemacolin's Path toward the Redstone Creek and its confluence with the Monongahela.

Halfway there, they had word from the Half King, a pro-English Seneca chief, that an advance party of French were encamped nearby, en route to seize them. Colonel Washington decided to strike first. He started off with forty men, met the Half King and his warriors, and with him planned a joint attack. In the early morning of May 28, they crept up on the French and surprised them completely. Their officer,

Fort Duquesne, built on the site of Virginia's Fort Prince George, later to be Fort Pitt and Pittsburgh.

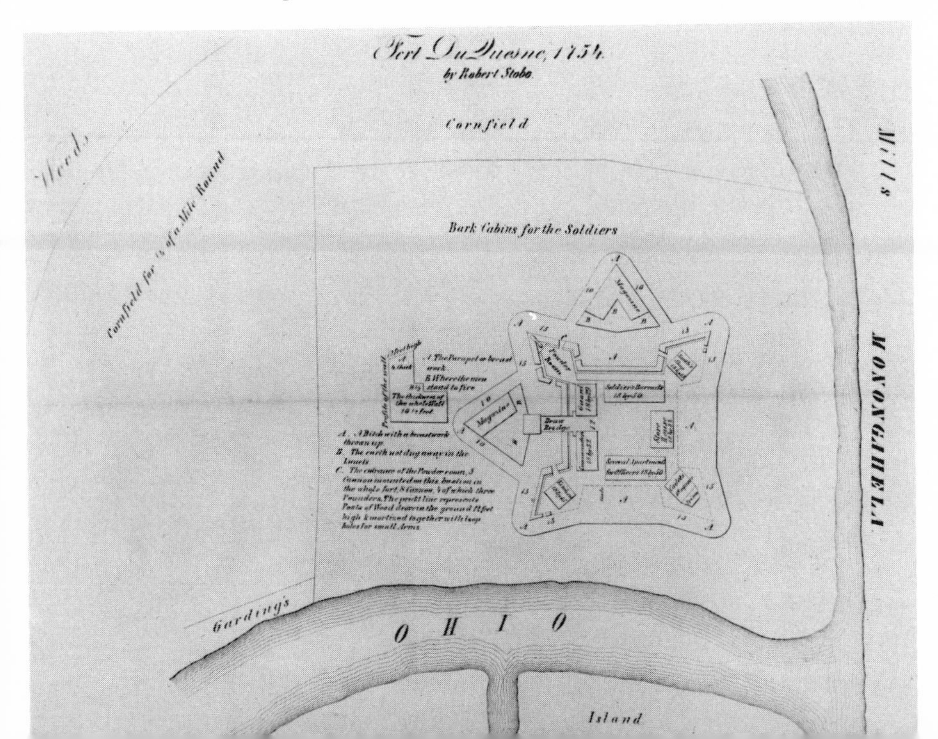

Washington and his men, holed up in Fort Necessity and surrounded by superior numbers, decide to surrender.

Ensign Joseph Coulon de Jumonville, was killed along with nine of his men, and twenty-two men were taken prisoner. One Canadian escaped to carry word back to Fort Duquesne.

Up to this moment, the duel over the Ohio Valley had been a private struggle between Virginia and Canada. But Washington's skirmish set off what would eventually become a worldwide conflict. "The volley fired by this young Virginian in the forests of America," wrote Horace Walpole, "has set the world in flames."

Defeat at Great Meadows

In the meantime, the twenty-two-year-old colonel had his own problems. He sent his prisoners back to Williamsburg and resumed his march toward the Redstone, widening and improving the road as he went. Some reinforcements reached him, a mere hundred men or so. Then in mid-June, when provisions were running low anyway, he received word that the French were coming for him with a large detachment of soldiers. By then Colonel Fry was dead of a fall from a horse, and it was plain that ample support could not be expected any time soon. So Washington turned around and retreated.

He had meant to return all the way to Wills Creek, but his men were too exhausted to draw the swivels through the mountains. Instead, they holed up in a rough fortification previously erected in a broad valley called Great Meadows (near modern Farmington, Pennsylvania). They had named the place Fort Necessity. The French found them there on July 3 and at about eleven in the morning opened up with musketry.

After a long rainy day of sniping, the French commander suggested a truce. If the Virginians surrendered and promised to return the May 28 prisoners, they would be allowed to march out with everything but their swivels. With thirty men dead and seventy wounded, powder wet and provisions low, Washington didn't have much choice. He signed the terms of surrender.

What he didn't know was that his interpreter was incompetent and had allowed him to admit that he had murdered Coulon de Jumonville. (The French commander at Fort Necessity was the dead ensign's half brother.) The French were later to use this admission against the British in propaganda campaigns in Europe. In any event, Washington returned to Williamsburg somewhat disgraced and resigned from the militia.

Edward Braddock Arrives

The British government was not yet ready to declare all-out war on France, but it had been sufficiently aroused by news of French actions to send regular troops to expel them from the Ohio Valley. The 44th and 48th Regiments of Foot were dispatched to Virginia under the command of Major General Edward Braddock.

The colonists were requested to contribute money and supplies, wagons and horses, and to furnish what troops they could. But, as usual, each colony—like Virginia in King George's War—volunteered help only to the degree she felt threatened. When Braddock landed at Alexandria, February 23, 1755, he found nothing had been done. Supplies promised had not been delivered, recruiting was slow. It took until May 9 to get the British troops to Wills Creek, where Fort Cumberland had now been built.

There Braddock was joined by some of the long-awaited supply wagons, two independent companies of regulars from New York, and about a thousand American troops, chiefly militia from Virginia and Carolina, plus some Pennsylvania volunteers. He liked the looks of the militia so little that he stationed them firmly in the rear of his line of march. He thought even less of about a hundred Indian allies and treated them with such disdain that most of them deserted.

When Benjamin Franklin warned him that his greatest danger would be from the Indians, not the French, he is reputed to have scoffed: "These savages may indeed be a formidable enemy to your raw American militia, but upon the King's regular and disciplined troops, sir, it is impossible they should make any impression."

Franklin was present at Wills Creek because he was instrumental in getting Braddock his supply wagons. Washington, clad in a deerhide hunting shirt, was there because he was acting as Braddock's civilian aide—Young Buckskins, the general called him. They weren't the only later-to-be-famous personages engaged in the enterprise. Captain Horatio Gates commanded the New York regulars, Captain Charles Lee led a company of the 44th, and Daniel Morgan served as a civilian wagoner —all to be American generals in the Revolution. Lieutenant Colonel Thomas Gage, later to dispatch troops to Lexington and Concord, now commanded the van, and it is thought that Daniel Boone took part as a young scout.

On June 7, Braddock left Wills Creek with over two thousand soldiers and headed up Nemacolin's Path, roadmaking as he went to get his heavy guns through. For many years thereafter, the route (roughly, modern US 40 and 119) was called Braddock's Road. They advanced only three to six miles a day, so that it was July 8 before they camped within reach of the fort.

Armed with bayonets and clad in red coats, the long line of Braddock's men winds along the forest path.

To the French, who had retained a bare five hundred men in Fort Duquesne, this seemed a perfect juggernaut rolling down on them. When a few officers volunteered to go out with half the garrison and waylay the oncoming British, the commandant only gave his consent as a forlorn hope. Nevertheless, six hundred Indians—some local Shawnee and Mingo as well as the Great Lakes tribesmen the French had brought with them—agreed to join the 250 or so French and Canadians. They knew just the spot for an ambush.

It was July 9, early afternoon, about eight miles from the fort. To avoid a narrow stretch, where the road was squeezed between the Monongahela and a steep bluff, Braddock's army forded the river, marched awhile on the southwest bank, then forded back. They had just made the second crossing, and the vanguard was mounting a gradual slope, when the two armies came briefly face to face. (The French had meant to catch them while in the act of fording and were late.) The men in the British van fired, and some of the French and Indians went down. The rest dived into the woods on either side of the road, where they opened a galling and accurate fire.

American settlers had long since learned that there were two things it was fatal to do when attacked by Indians in the woods—one was to stand still, and the other was to run. Unfortunately, the regulars did both.

The correct course, if you survived the first volley, was to get behind something—preferably with a partner, so you could keep one another covered while reloading—and then hold out. Indians liked swift, overwhelming victory; if winning was made difficult, they got bored after a while and went home. With this in mind, the Virginia troops melted into the woods and, as a result, were the only men still alive and actively firing at the enemy three hours later.

No eighteenth-century king's officer could order his men to take cover in battle, of course, but there was one order Colonel Gage could have given that might have saved the day: "Fix bayonets and charge." A swift and vigorous assault might have so disconcerted the Indians that they would have scattered, leaving the French to face the main body of British troops. Moreover, charging men are much harder to panic than men halted or in retreat. But Gage didn't think fast enough and instead gave the worst order possible: "Halt."

The men halted, fired a volley. When that brought only an answering fire from assailants still unseen, they wavered. Their officers rallied them, got a feeble second volley out of them, and then the regulars broke and ran. They collided with the oncoming main body, communicated their panic to them, and soon had the entire army falling all over itself to escape. In vain officers tried to rally them, cursed, threatened, even ran some through—the men were insane with panic and would not heed. Some of those who could get clear dashed off into the woods, where they were easily run down and dispatched by the Indians. Twelve were taken prisoner and dragged off to Duquesne to be tortured. The rest simply milled about in struggling confusion, with the artillery and baggage trains blocking the road, presenting a superb red target for the French.

The mortally wounded Braddock is carried from the field to die not far from Fort Necessity.

The officers, who stayed to fight, suffered worst—out of sixty who came under fire, only five remained unwounded. One of these was George Washington who, as the official report stated, "had two horses shot under him and his clothes shot through in several places, behaving the whole time with the greatest courage and resolution." * Gates and Gage were both wounded. Braddock had five horses shot under him and at last was wounded himself, fatally.

The survivors saw it was no use, and a retreat was ordered—back across the Monongahela, back by way of the newly made road to the supply base at Great Meadows, where Braddock died, back across the mountains to Wills Creek. There, Braddock's second-in-command took the remnants of the troops off to Philadelphia, deserting the Ohio entirely.

* In 1770, while visiting his Ohio Valley lands, Washington was approached by an old Indian who told him through an interpreter that he had been present that day at the Monongahela. He had repeatedly had Washington in his gun sights, he said, and had repeatedly missed. He had concluded therefore that Washington's manitou was too strong for his and that the Virginian would never be killed in battle. Perhaps he was right—Washington had *something* going for him.

It was a defeat and a disgrace for British arms. It was a disaster for Virginia.

Border War

The colony's frontiers were now wide open to raids by the victorious Indians. Attacking almost everywhere during 1755 and 1756, they drove settlers back across the Blue Ridge in such numbers that in the spring of 1756 the Shenandoah Valley seemed deserted.

The House of Burgesses hastily voted money for militia to protect the settlements that were left. Governor Dinwiddie reappointed George Washington commander of the colony's armed forces with his old rank of colonel.

Despite the dangers, Washington still found volunteers scarce. By the end of 1755, he had only half as many men as he needed, and even those were the hard-drinking, badly disciplined forces that the frontier usually produced. He did what he could with this little army, dividing the men up among a line of sixteen stockade forts, which had been hastily built along a four-hundred-mile frontier from the Potomac nearly to North Carolina. He rode ceaselessly from one to another, trying to infuse the men with some of his own energy and strength of purpose.

For two years Washington held frontier Virginia together. Then, overcome with dysentery, he was ordered home for his health. That was at the end of 1757, and by then it no longer mattered so much. For William Pitt was prime minister, Great Britain was at war with France, and the second campaign against Fort Duquesne was about to be launched.

John Forbes Arrives

The war that sprang to life in the Allegheny Mountains of backwoods America spread to the continent of Europe, where it touched off a furious conflict between beleaguered Prussia and an encirclement of enemies: Russia, Sweden, Austria, Saxony, and France. Because France was fighting on one side, England allied herself with Frederick the Great on the other. Soon the French and the British were clashing in the Mediterranean, the Indian Ocean, India itself, Africa, the West Indies.

At first things went badly for England. Expeditions were botched, losses heavy. Then popular demand in England forced the king to relinquish the conduct of government to William Pitt, a man he hated and had always managed to keep out of office. Pitt was a master of efficient statecraft, and almost at once the tide turned. He concentrated his conduct of the war on France's overseas dominions, starting with Canada.

Expeditions were sent against Louisburg on Cape Breton and against the French forts on Lake Champlain. And in May, 1758, doughty Brigadier John Forbes was assigned to move against the Forks.

Washington's Virginia forces were ordered to join the expedition, their commander–now recovered–with them. Instead of proceeding by way of Braddock's old route, Forbes decided to cut a new road through Pennsylvania (roughly, modern US 30), because the route was somewhat shorter and supplies were more readily available in the Quaker province than in Virginia. It was slow work, and by early September they were still forty miles from Fort Duquesne. A scouting expedition of Scots regulars, sent ahead, was caught and overpowered just outside the fort. General Forbes was dying of an exhausting and painful illness and had to be carried nearly the whole distance in a horse litter, but when it was suggested that the troops go into winter quarters in November, the sick man would not hear of it.

Doggedly the expedition pushed on through constant rain, mired in slick clay on the slopes of Laurel Hill. Washington, who had advised against building the new road, was filled with gloomy foreboding, but for once he was proved wrong. By late November the expedition passed Chestnut Ridge, the last of the great Appalachian heights. One night, from the direction of the Forks, they heard an explosion. The next day an advance party under Washington arrived to find Fort Duquesne blown up and the French gone off down the Ohio to the Mississippi. Two days later Forbes wrote to Pitt:

Washington raises the British ensign over fallen Fort Duquesne, climax of a long, arduous campaign.

Pittsbourgh, 27th Novem^{r}, 1758

Sir,

I do myself the Honour of acquainting you that it has pleased God to crown His Majesty's Arms with Success over all His Enemies upon the Ohio. . . . I have used the freedom of giving your name to Fort Du Quesne, as I hope it was in some measure the being actuated by your spirits that now makes us Masters of the place. . . .

One by one other French citadels in the New World fell, and in the treaty of Paris, signed February, 1763, all of Canada was ceded to

Great Britain. But Virginia's primary concern in the conflict was the Ohio Valley, and she did not interest herself strongly in the later campaigns. Even Pontiac's Rising in the summer of 1763—the most widespread and nearly successful of all Indian revolts—had little effect on her, because its brunt was borne by the king's regular troops occupying the Great Lakes and other frontier forts.

John Forbes died, Robert Dinwiddie resigned, and George Washington retired from the militia to marry and settle down at Mount Vernon (on his journeys to and from the Ohio, he had met a pretty widow). Washington had done his public duty, he felt. Now he could live out the rest of his life in peaceful obscurity.

He wasn't the only one to misread the temper of the times.

CHAPTER NINE

Security Against a Burthensome Taxation

Now that Great Britain had won control of the continent she was faced with the problem of paying for her conquest. The war had left her with a large debt. Moreover, if the vast new lands were to be protected, garrisons would have to be maintained at a scattering of forts. Since the chief benefactors from the war had been Americans and these forts were for the protection of American settlers, it seemed only right and just that Americans should help to pay for them.

Accordingly, the Navigation Acts were strengthened by the Sugar Act of 1764. This legislation greatly raised customs duties in a number of different ways, affecting particularly the intercolonial trade in molasses and rum. It tightened up shipping regulations and curtailed the right of trial by jury by turning customs-seizure cases over to courts of admiralty. The act also included a hint that the government meant to pass a stamp act the following year.

Virginia, like other colonies, accepted Parliament's right to collect duties on exports and imports as a means of regulating the trade of the empire. But a stamp tax would be a direct tax on the colony's internal business, which Virginians felt was the exclusive right of their own General Assembly to levy. A ground swell of alarm ran through the colonies, to which Virginia responded.

Resolutions protesting the proposed stamp tax were drawn up by colony after colony. Virginia's read in part:

"We conceive it to be a fundamental Principal of the British Constitution, without which Freedom can no Where exist, that the People are not subject to any taxes but such as are laid on them by their own Consent."

Embodying this principle in petitions to king and Parliament, Virginia made a formal protest against the proposed tax, as did many of her sister colonies.

The following May the House of Burgesses was winding up its spring session when word came that Parliament had, after all, passed the Stamp Act. The act provided that fifteen different kinds of documents could be printed only on paper that carried an official government stamp. College diplomas, licenses of many kinds, indenture bonds, deeds, wills, ship's manifests and customs cockets, even newspapers and almanacs had to use stamped paper. Thus there was scarcely any aspect of life on which the Stamp Act would not lay a tax.

As for the colonial petitions, they had not even been considered by Parliament.

Many of the 116 burgesses, dismayed by the news and despondent, abandoned the session and went home. The rest, sitting as a committee of the whole house, took up the Stamp Act question. There were only thirty-nine members present when one of their number got to his feet and proposed a set of resolutions. His name was Patrick Henry, and though he had only been a burgess nine days, he already had a reputation as an orator.

The Virginia Resolves

Henry was one of the "new breed"—a Hanover County Scot who spoke for the common man. His rise to fame was almost symbolic of the backcountry settlers' taking their due share of power in the colony. He had won his name in the notorious Parsons' Cause.

The king had vetoed an act of the House of Burgesses which had decreed that any debt incurred in tobacco could be discharged at the rate of 2*d* a pound. This veto had been brought about largely by the clergy, who wanted to continue selling their tobacco salaries on the open market, and one of them, the Reverend James Maury, sued the colony

Patrick Henry, orator from the back country, so fired his fellow Virginians that they passed the strong Resolves.

to settle the legal date that it went into effect. He won. A second trial was then set to determine the damages he was to collect, and Patrick Henry was hired to plead the tithepayers' side.

For openers, he called the clergymen "rapacious harpies . . . who would snatch from the hearth of their honest parishioner his last hoecake!" Then he lighted into the king. The monarch's veto, he said, was the act of a tyrant who "forfeits all rights to his subjects' obedience," for the House of Burgesses represented the will of the people of Virginia.

This was strong stuff, challenging political concepts as old as Virginia herself. It brought cries of "Treason! Treason!" from some of Henry's less avid auditors. But it won the case. Maury was awarded damages of a single penny, and Henry was carried off on the people's shoulders.

Now, with a denunciation of the king under his belt, Henry was ready to take on Parliament. He proposed that the House of Burgesses pass a flat statement of Virginians' rights as Englishmen.

The resolutions were hotly debated by the thirty-nine. Such representatives of Tidewater Virginia as Peyton Randolph, George Wythe, and Edmund Pendleton were aghast at the thought of making any stand so impudent as a denial of Parliamentary authority. But Patrick Henry argued passionately for passage, and Henry was a man whose every word, wrote his contemporary George Mason, "not only engages but commands the attention."

"Tarquin and Caesar each had his Brutus!" he cried, working his way to a climax. "Charles the First his Cromwell! And George the Third—"

"Treason!" the Speaker cautioned him. But Henry had heard cries of "Treason" before.

"And George the Third may profit by their example! If this be treason, make the most of it!"

His eloquence carried the day. Five of his seven resolutions were passed. Later, one was rescinded, and only four remained on the journals of the house. But they were unequivocal statements of conviction:

> *Resolved*, That the first adventurers and Settlers of this his Majesty's Colony and Dominion of *Virginia* brought with them, and transmitted to their Posterity, and all other his Majesty's Subjects since inhabiting in this his Majesty's said Colony, all the Liberties, Privileges, Franchises, and Immunities, that have at any Time been held, enjoyed, and possessed, by the people of *Great Britain*.
>
> *Resolved*, That by two royal Charters, granted by King *James* the First, the Colonists aforesaid are declared entitled to all Liberties, Privileges, and Immunities of Denizens and natural Subjects, to all Intents and Purposes as if they had been abiding and born within the Realm of *England*.
>
> *Resolved*, That the Taxation of the People by themselves, or by Persons chosen by themselves to represent them, who can only know what Taxes the People are able to bear, or the easiest Method of raising them, and must themselves be affected by every Tax laid on the People, is the only Security against a burthensome Taxation, and the distinguishing Characteristick of *British* Freedom, without which the ancient Constitution cannot exist.
>
> *Resolved*, That his Majesty's liege People of this his most ancient and loyal Colony have without Interruption enjoyed the inesti-

mable Right of being governed by such Laws, respecting their internal Polity and Taxation, as are derived from their own Consent, with the Approbation of their Sovereign, or his Substitute; and that the same hath never been forfeited or yielded up, but hath been constantly recognized by the Kings and People of *Great Britain.*

These Virginia Resolves had a wide circulation throughout the colonies and were met with prideful acclaim. Massachusetts called for a Stamp Act Congress—the colonies to elect special representatives to meet in New York in October to work out a joint resolution. Virginia was prevented from joining this convention by her governor, Francis Fauquier, who refused to convene an assembly to elect representatives, but the Resolves spoke for her, and their language had a strong influence on the twelve-article declaration that resulted.

Attacks on the Stamp Distributors

Resolutions and speechmaking were not enough for the angry colonists, however. They determined to make it hot for anyone who attempted to put the provisions of the Stamp Act into action. This meant particularly the officially appointed distributors of stamped paper. There was one for every colony, and they were nearly all native Americans, which made it easy to get at them. Hotheaded Boston struck first.

On August 14, the Massachusetts stamp distributor was hanged in effigy from the Liberty Tree, and his house was ransacked and smashed by a mob. Under pressure, he agreed to resign his office. Two weeks later Newport acted, and the same thing happened to the Rhode Island distributor. The distributors of New York and New Jersey resigned as soon as they heard the news from Boston. Maryland's distributor had his house wrecked on September 2 and fled for his life. Connecticut and New Hampshire resigned a few days later, Pennsylvania in early October, and the two Carolinas on October 20 and 27.

The distributor for Virginia, George Mercer, was in England at the time of his appointment. He arrived in Williamsburg on Wednesday,

Cartoon lampooning American methods of coercing officials by threatening them with violence.

October 30, two days before the unpopular measure was to go into effect and—unfortunately for him—during one of the Publick Times. He headed for Mrs. Campbell's tavern, where he intended to lodge, but before he had even arrived there, he was confronted by a large, indignant street crowd demanding he resign his position. Governor Fauquier, who witnessed the scene from the porch of the tavern, wrote that he would have called the gathering a mob "did I not know that it was chiefly if not altogether composed of gentlemen of property in the Colony, some of them at the head of their respective Counties."

The bewildered Mercer asked for time to talk things over with his friends. "I'll give you an answer by ten o'clock Friday. Meet me at the Capitol steps."

"Friday is too late. The act takes place then."

Mercer managed to reach the porch of the tavern, but the crowd hung about, surly, demanding that he give his answer by the following day. "I've already given an answer," the distributor retorted.

The anger of the crowd increased. There were mutterings of "Let's rush in." The leaders began to push up the steps, and the governor, fearing for the distributor's safety, stepped up to his side.

At that the mob fell back. Fauquier, a man of great ability, elegance, and tact, was immensely popular in Virginia, and though the crowd lingered and "there was some murmurs," they made no attempt to harm Mercer. Finally he agreed to give his answer the following day.

The governor escorted him through the midst of the crowd to the Palace, where the two men discussed the problem. Fauquier felt it his duty to urge Mercer to stand firm, but the man's father and brother were equally insistent that he not be foolhardy. He returned to Mrs. Campbell's still uncertain.

The next day a great crowd—augmented by country people brought in overnight—gathered at the Capitol to hear Mercer's decision. Mercer arrived and read a formal statement: "I will not, directly or indirectly, by myself or deputies, proceed in the execution of the act. . . ."

He was cheered by the crowd. That night, every window in Williamsburg was illuminated, and the citizens rejoiced in a holiday mood.

The Declaratory Act

With this act of defiance, the campaign opened. Ships were sent to sea without stamped clearance papers, but courts were kept closed. People signed articles of association by which they pledged not to use stamps and not to import English goods. The trade boycott, combined with the closing of the courts (suits could not be entered to collect debts), caused a sharp profit pinch in England almost immediately, and this was passed on to the workingman in the shape of unemployment. The panicky British merchants began to pressure Parliament to repeal the act before they were ruined altogether.

The following winter, a new faction took over in Parliament, and the Stamp Act was repealed. However, repeal was accompanied by a Declaratory Act that stated that Parliament had "full power and authority to make laws and statutes of sufficient force and validity to bind the colonists and people of America, subjects of the crown of Great Britain, in all cases whatsoever."

The colonists paid little attention to this ominous note and fell instead into universal rejoicing. Part of this was attributable to affection and good feeling for the mother country, but just as much of it was motivated by pride in their newfound unity and power. For the quarrel with Parliament had done what threats of war with the Indians and the French had never been able to do—brought them to cooperate with one another and speak with one voice.

Let Parliament do her worst! They could always organize another boycott!

The Townshend Acts

Another boycott was exactly what would soon be needed, for in 1767 Parliament adopted the Townshend Acts, which established a board of customs to control smuggling and levied import duties on certain items: glass, paper, painters' colors, and tea.

In some ways this was a much cleverer enactment than the Stamp Act. It turned the colonists' own argument about internal-versus-external taxation against them. Moreover, it didn't affect everyone equally, and therefore not everyone was angered by it. Nonetheless, passage of the Townshend Acts was the action that would in the end drive Americans to independence.

But first they did the things they had done before. In April, 1768, the House of Burgesses sent three memorials to London, claiming, as the Resolves had done, that "no power on Earth has a Right to impose Taxes upon the People . . . without their Consent. . . ." The royal governors were under orders to dissolve colonial assemblies that passed such inflammatory measures, but Fauquier had just died, so Virginia escaped prorogation for the moment. The following May, however, Norborne Berkeley, Baron de Botetourt—a distant relation of Sir William Berkeley—was seated in the Palace. When another set of such resolutions was voted for, his lordship prorogued the House.

The burgesses left the Capitol and walked up Duke of Gloucester Street to the Raleigh Tavern. In the Apollo Room, where public balls were held, they met as private citizens and formed a nonimportation agreement, binding themselves to boycott British goods until the obnoxious duties were removed.

One participant in this affair, serving his first term as burgess, was twenty-six-year-old Thomas Jefferson. Jefferson was an unusual combination of backcountry and Tidewater. His mother was a Randolph, and his father, though not rich, came of a family that had been in Virginia since 1619. But Thomas was raised in Albemarle County, in the Piedmont. His father, himself uneducated, had insisted that his son have a strict classical education and train for the law, and after attending William and Mary, young Thomas served five years in the offices of George Wythe. Tall, gangling, sandy-haired, and sweet-tempered, he was to combine in his thinking and writing the passionate democracy of the frontier with the literate grace of elegant Tidewater.

Hanging Fire

Between 1769 and 1773, the question of colonial rights hung fire. Nonimportation agreements were hard to enforce over the long run. A man caught putting new windows in his house could always claim the glass had been smuggled in from Holland, and no one could prove otherwise. Patriotic fervor had a way of waning, and men got bored with the long round of drawing up petitions to which nobody ever listened. After 1770, when Parliament removed the duty on everything except tea, many people lost interest in the abstract question of rights. Only the official committees of correspondence, which passed news from one colony to another, kept the cause alive—aided from time to time by some notorious collision between colonists and customs men.

Then in 1773 the London government granted special license to the East India Company to carry several shiploads of their stockpiled tea directly to the colonies. It was intended as a leg-up for the nearly bankrupt company, but the ministers also hoped that the cheapness of the product would cause it to sell, duty and all, thus breaking the boycott.

Virginia was not directly interested in the tea imports, because they went to the major port cities. Besides, just about that time, her attention was drawn inland once more. Now it was Pennsylvania laying claim to the Forks of the Ohio!

Clashing Claims

Pennsylvania's charter provided that her western boundary was to be a north-south line five degrees of longitude west of the Delaware. The line had never been surveyed, but Pennsylvania claimed that Pittsburgh lay well within it, and Virginia claimed it didn't. Virginia had fought for the Forks when Pennsylvania had been reluctant; many Virginians had migrated to the region under the impression that their colony's jurisdiction extended that far. Pennsylvania, on the other hand, had bought the land from the Indians. Now she was setting up a new county west of the mountains and taking steps to make her hold on the region permanent. Virginia's governor dispatched a representative to do the same thing for Virginia.

John Murray, fourth Earl of Dunmore and Virginia's last royal governor, a stocky, tactless man.

Virginia had had extraordinary good luck in her eighteenth-century governors. Spotswood, Sir William Gooch, Dinwiddie, Fauquier, and Botetourt had all been able, sensible men with the good of the colony at heart. The colony was long overdue for a lemon, and in 1771 she got one: John Murray, fourth Earl of Dunmore.

Dunmore was a stocky, tactless man who loved dogs but did not think much of Virginians and was given to acting in haste and repenting in leisure. He had acquired large land holdings in the back country, and when he heard about Pennsylvania's move, he leaped to protect his investment. He found a former army surgeon named John Connolly, who had excellent frontier connections, and sent him—about two weeks after the Boston Sons of Liberty had climbed aboard the *Dartmouth*, the *Eleanor*, and the *Beaver*, and dumped 342 chests of Bohea tea into Boston Harbor—to Pittsburgh to establish Virginia's jurisdiction.

Connolly set about his assignment boldly. Arriving in Pittsburgh, he issued a call for militia—an illegal act in Pennsylvania—and when the Pennsylvania magistrates took him to court, he had three of them arrested and carried off to Winchester. His followers were the rowdy frontiersmen who had come up from Virginia to settle, and since he sold land at half the price the Penns charged for it, he won many Pennsylvania adherents to his side as well. He could do about as he pleased, because Pennsylvania had no militia with which to protect her citizens.

The Penns protested to Lord Dunmore. He agreed, though reluctantly, to submit the matter to London. In the meantime he encouraged Connolly to sell as much land as possible as fast as possible, in case the decision should go against Virginia. He made no attempt to restrain Connolly's highhandedness.

Throughout the early months of 1774, Connolly kept the region in turmoil, continually announcing that trouble was brewing with the Indians. It was one of those self-fulfilling prophecies, for the alarmed whites began to get their licks in first. The most notorious of these "incidents" was the slaughter of the entire family of the friendly Mingo chief, Logan, who were lured by twos and threes from their village to a white man's trading post on the opposite side of the Ohio and wantonly murdered.

Not unnaturally, there was an Indian uprising. All across the frontier isolated cabins were attacked, the settlers slain. Many fled the region altogether or to the protection of forts—forting, it was called. Connolly sent to his master for help.

Lord Dunmore's War

It was Dunmore's chance to put Virginia's claim beyond question, or so he seemed to feel. He called up the militia of the frontier counties, divided them into two sections, and put himself in command of one section and Andrew Lewis, an experienced frontier fighter who had served with Forbes, in command of the other. Dunmore then went to Pittsburgh to take charge of his half, and ordered Lewis to rendezvous with him at the confluence of the Ohio and the Kanawha rivers. He planned to attack the Shawnee villages in the Ohio country.

Colonel Lewis reached the place appointed (modern Point Pleasant, West Virginia) on October 1, 1774. No Dunmore. On October 9, Lewis learned that the governor had gone directly down the Ohio in boats and now wanted Lewis's force to join him at the Scioto River. But early the following morning, before he could break camp, eight hundred Shawnee crept up on him. They were led by their principal chief, Cornstalk, who hoped to panic and scatter the Virginians in traditional fashion and thus start a general withdrawal all across the frontier. But Lewis held out, and a ferocious, all-day battle ensued, with both sides giving and taking in about equal proportions. At length Cornstalk saw that he could not win and, as night fell, the Indians withdrew.

After taking a brief respite to pull his command together, Lewis continued on to the Scioto, where a council was called and peace dictated to the Indians. It was at this meeting that Logan made a speech that was to become a favorite recitation piece of American schoolchildren.

> I appeal to any white man to say if he ever entered Logan's cabin hungry, and he gave him not meat; if ever he came cold and naked, and he clothed him not. . . . I had even thought

> to have lived with you, but for the injuries of one man [who] last spring in cold blood and unprovoked, murdered all the relations of Logan, not sparing even my women and children. There runs not a drop of my blood in the veins of any living creature. . . . Who is there to mourn for Logan? Not one.

Pleased with himself, Lord Dunmore marched home, where he was hailed as a victor, and set about the much less congenial task of subduing the increasingly rebellious colonists.

The First Continental Congress

While the frontier people had been occupied with this minidrama, Parliament had been preparing punishment for Boston over destruction of the tea. The Boston Port Bill closed the port, saddled the city with occupying troops, and took local government entirely out of the colonists' hands. It also united the bickering colonies against the mother country, out of sympathy for the martyred city.

Virginia was quick to come to the aid of Boston by sending food and other supplies. On May 24, 1774, a resolution was introduced in the House of Burgesses that June 1 (the day the Port Bill was to go into effect) be set aside as a day of fasting, humiliation, and prayer, "devoutly to implore the divine interposition, for averting the heavy Calamity which threatens destruction of our Civil Rights. . . ." The resolution passed and was printed up, and two days later the burgesses were summoned to the Council chamber.

Lord Dunmore waved the printed resolution and said it "makes it necessary for me to dissolve you, and you are dissolved accordingly."

Again the burgesses gathered unofficially in the Apollo Room at the Raleigh and signed another pledge of association not to import English goods. They also proposed that a congress of all the colonies should meet in Philadelphia. When word was received that other colonies were also eager for such a meeting, the burgesses issued a call for a convention to choose Virginia's delegates.

The convention met in August and chose Peyton Randolph, Richard Bland, Benjamin Harrison, Patrick Henry, Richard Henry Lee, Edmund Pendleton, and George Washington. All except Henry and Pendleton represented the planter class and might have been expected to side conservatively with the home government. But they were men accustomed to ruling themselves, and most of them were coming to believe, with Patrick Henry, that self-rule was dangerously jeopardized by Parliament's actions. Even so, they did reject as too radical the instructions proposed for them by Thomas Jefferson. He would have had them deny Parliament all authority whatsoever.

These instructions were so powerfully stated that they were published in pamphlet form with the title *A Summary View of the Rights of British America.* The pamphlet was sent to England and widely distributed, but like most other American productions, it impressed only those members of Parliament who were already favorable to the American cause. However, it made Jefferson's name as a writer of political documents.

The First Continental Congress opened September 5, 1774, in Carpenters' Hall, Philadelphia. It recommended that local committees be established throughout the colonies to enforce the ban against all commerce with Great Britain. The local committees were to publish the names of merchants who continued to import English goods and force them to obey the nonimportation agreements or be branded public enemies. Addresses were prepared and sent to the king and to the peoples of Great Britain, Quebec, and the British colonies—but not, deliberately, to Parliament. A general declaration of rights was written, emphasizing that the colonists did not want to revolt—that is, to overthrow their present governments and set up new ones—but to return to the way things had been before the Sugar Act. That done, Congress took up the Suffolk Resolves—a Massachusetts proposal that the colonies arm themselves and train in preparation for war.

That suggestion gave many of the delegates pause. It was one thing to declare rights and draw up petitions to the king. But to prepare to make out-and-out war on the mother country—that was another affair altogether. Nevertheless, the Congress passed the Resolves.

The House once again closed, the burgesses returned to the Raleigh to sign new pledges not to import.

On October 26 the First Continental Congress came to a close, and the delegates departed for home to try to implement its decisions. Virginians called a second convention to meet the following March, 1775, at St. John's Church in Richmond. There delegates were chosen for the Second Continental Congress in May.

Most men had good hope, despite the Suffolk Resolves, that agreement could be reached with Great Britain and Boston extricated from her troubles. But Patrick Henry, ever the firebrand, believed Virginia should prepare for the worst. When the convention met, he introduced a resolution calling for the "embodying, arming, and disciplining" of the colonial militia. When his plan met opposition from most of the powerful leaders of the convention, Henry leaped to his feet and launched himself into the speech every schoolboy knows:

> Gentlemen may cry, peace, peace—but there is no peace. The war is actually begun! The next gale that sweeps from the north will bring to our ears the clash of resounding arms! Our brethren are already in the field! Why stand we here idle? What is it that gentlemen wish? What would they have? Is life so dear, or peace so sweet, as to be purchased at the price of chains and slavery? Forbid it, Almighty God! I know not what course others may take, but as for me, give me liberty, or give me death!

The delegates sat stunned. Then, pulling themselves together, they voted for Henry's motion.

A month later, news came from beleaguered Boston: Regular troops, marching out to seize powder and stores at Concord, had been set upon by the Massachusetts militia and chased back to the city in a hail of bullets. The war for independence had begun.

CHAPTER TEN

The World Turned Upside Down

The war began for Virginia with an incident similar to Concord's. Lord Dunmore had been agitated by the warlike proceedings in Richmond and thought he had better remove the powder from the Williamsburg magazine. He called on the navy for help—there was always a warship or two hanging about Chesapeake Bay and the rivers, looking for smugglers—and was sent a detachment of marines. Dunmore kept them hidden at the Palace until the coast should be clear, which happened on the night of April 20–21, 1775. They slipped out under cover of darkness, seized the powder, and were in the act of spiriting it off when the alarm was given.

Williamsburg erupted. Bells were rung, militia summoned, the town was in an uproar. A crowd gathered before the courthouse and threatened the governor's life. But the marines got away with the powder and took it by schooner to H.M. frigate *Fowey*, a man-of-war at anchor in Hampton Roads.

Peyton Randolph and some others were successful in calming the hotheads, and instead of an armed assault on the Palace—as the now unprotected governor feared—the mayor of the town approached with a written petition requesting that the powder be returned. Dunmore refused to order the powder brought back and gave as his excuse that he wanted to avoid letting it fall into the hands of rebellious slaves. If the powder was needed in an emergency, he said, it would be returned within half an hour—an answer that fell rather short of the truth, since the barrels were already halfway to Norfolk.

Dunmore confronts the citizens of Williamsburg, angered because he has carried off their powder.

When the mayor had to report this refusal, the crowd became unruly again. But short of actually seizing the governor's person—and despite the big talk they had not yet brought themselves to that pitch—there was nothing they could do. They hung about the streets for the most part, muttering threats.

Dunmore barricaded himself in the Palace and debated whether or not to arm his slaves. (He also considered arming some Shawnee hostages he'd brought back from the Ohio.) When a local physician made a professional call on the household the following day, the governor fumed to him that he had half a mind to "declare Freedom to the slaves and reduce the City of Williamsburg to ashes."

Meanwhile, a large body of horsemen gathered at Fredericksburg prepared to move on the capital. Some of the militia in Williamsburg marched out to join them, and messengers sped into all the neighboring counties to rouse other units. But things gradually quieted down in Williamsburg, so Peyton Randolph, about to set out for Philadelphia and the Second Congress, sent word to the militia that they should disperse. This was done, but shortly thereafter yet another body of armed men threatened to descend on Williamsburg—the Hanover County militia, with none other than Patrick Henry himself at their head.

This news was too much for the rattled governor. He sent his wife and children off to the *Fowey* and summoned another detachment of marines to protect him.

Their services were unneeded, however, because cooler heads among colonial officials prevailed on Henry to accept payment for the powder in lieu of its return. This caused the governor to issue a proclamation urging people "not to aid, abet, or give Countenance to the said Patrick Henry" and giving, as one reason for this, Henry's "extorting from His Majesty's Receiver General the Sum of £330, under Pretence of replacing the Powder. . . ."

However, by the middle of May it had all blown over. Henry was free to go off to Philadelphia to the Congress, the governor dismissed the marines, and Lady Dunmore came ashore from the *Fowey*.

The Governor Flees

Lord Dunmore called the General Assembly into session on June 1 and laid before the burgesses proposals of conciliation that had been passed by Parliament the previous winter. If a colony would vote money for the defenses of the empire, in proportions satisfactory to king and Parliament, as well as provide fully for the support of its own local governments, that colony would be exempt from Parliamentary taxation—except such as would serve to regulate trade.

It had come too late. Many of the same men who had reacted in horror to the Virginia Resolves in 1765 were now, ten years later, beginning to think quite seriously of declaring independence. The House of Burgesses approved the acts of the Virginia convention and rejected the British offer as a bald attempt to drive a wedge between colony and colony.

But before the burgesses had a chance to inform the governor of their decision—they had an appointment to do so the following afternoon—

Lord Dunmore packed up his family and servants and fled in the middle of the night to the *Fowey*. Feckless to the end, he gave no reason for the timing of this move, alleging only that infuriated people might "work themselves up to that pitch of daringness and atrociousness as to fall upon me. . . ."

The astonished burgesses begged the governor to return, assuring him that he was in no danger. From first to last, Virginia had remained relatively calm, and there had not even been attacks on property as in other colonies. But Dunmore refused. Accordingly, when their work was finished, the burgesses took on themselves something that had hitherto been the sole prerogative of the governor: They adjourned.

In effect, it was the end of royal government in Virginia.

The Second Continental Congress

While this was taking place in Virginia, the Second Continental Congress was sitting at Philadelphia. It composed and sent the Olive Branch Petition to the king, begging him to "settle peace through every part of our Dominions." But the delegates had little hope of the petition working (it didn't, the king refused to hear it on the grounds that he would deal only with the colonies as individual provinces, not through an illegal union). So they also adopted the motley assortment of New England militia that had been besieging Boston ever since Lexington-Concord. Henceforth it would be regarded as a "continental army."

Then John Adams got up and proposed that one of the delegates present be named commander-in-chief of this force, "a gentleman of Virginia. . . ." Every eye swung toward George Washington, who had attended the Congress wearing his old militia uniform. He slipped out so that they could debate the choice without embarrassment. The following day they voted unanimously to approve the motion.

It had been the purest politics, an effort to bind southern sympathies to what had so far been a New England revolt. But by accident they had chosen the very man the situation needed. For there would be times in the dark and dangerous years ahead when the American cause would be

George Washington in the uniform of a lieutenant general in the Continental Army.

held together by almost nothing but the personal character of this one tall Virginian.

For the moment, Washington said little but packed up and hurried off to Boston, to be met on the road by a messenger carrying news of Bunker Hill. Congress continued its debates, trying to nerve itself to make the final move, to cut the final tie with the mother country.

Dunmore Gathers Strength

Meanwhile, Lord Dunmore was at it again. After leaving Williamsburg, he had lurked about Norfolk and Hampton, aboard first one warship and then another. Sometime during the summer his friend John Connolly conferred with him, and together they concerted plans to raise the king's standard on the frontier. However, Connolly was arrested en route to the Ohio and spent most of the war in a Philadelphia prison. (The boundary dispute was settled amicably in 1779 and the line laid out as it runs today.)

Slowly a little flotilla gathered to his lordship's support: three armed merchantmen, a frigate, three sloops-of-war, plus numerous smaller vessels. In August several companies of the 14th Foot were ordered to join him from Florida. With these men Dunmore conducted a series of nuisance raids all around Hampton Roads–seizing supplies from farmers, destroying military stores, confiscating the printing press of a newspaper that had belabored the governor, looting, taking possession of private vessels. On November 14, after a successful raid, he posted the long-warned-of notice:

"I do . . . declare all indentured servants, negroes, or others (appertaining to rebels) free, that are able and willing to bear arms, they joining his Majesty's troops as soon as may be. . . ."

One by one the blacks began to disappear, and Virginia took alarm–especially since Dunmore was ashore by now in Norfolk and fortifying the land approaches to the town at a marshy place called Great Bridge. The thought of slaves revolting–"servile insurrection" was the polite term–had always been Virginia's private nightmare, and now here was the erstwhile governor offering to arm any servants who ran off to him!

Battle of Great Bridge

Virginia's troops had been more and more active throughout the summer and fall of 1775, occasionally countering Dunmore raids and generally pulling their defenses together. Now his lordship's proclamation spurred them into going on the offensive. Counterfortifications were erected opposite Dunmore's at Great Bridge, where the road to Norfolk ran across a narrow causeway, and as soon as some North Carolina reinforcements arrived, Colonel William Woodford planned to assault the opposite lines.

Many of the Virginia troops had been imported from the frontier counties and were armed with the backcountry's weapon, the long rifle. Developed in 1727 by some unknown German gunsmith in Lancaster, Pennsylvania, this weapon had a rifled barrel that spun the bullet as it emerged, thus driving it in a much truer line than the smoothbore musket could achieve. Not only was the rifle accurate at twice the range of the regulation musket, with which the regulars were armed, but it fired a bullet less than half the size and thus was cheaper to operate. It could not be fitted with a bayonet, but the Virginians had no intention of letting the British come within bayonet reach of them anyway—a determination they amply demonstrated at Great Bridge on the morning of December 9, 1775.

For the British had heard that reinforcements were coming and had resolved to strike first. At dawn they moved out onto the causeway, six abreast, drums beating.

The Virginians were taken by surprise. A bare twenty-five men were in the trenches, and their first volley was ragged. But their officer got them under control, ordered them to hold their fire until the advancing redcoats were only fifty yards off. Then, "Fire!"

Bullets tore into the front rank of the British. Still, in true bulldog-breed fashion, they came on, volley after volley, until one or two were within touch of the Virginia breastworks. But by then the causeway was strewn with bodies, and the British commanding officer ordered a withdrawal. The officer who had led the van had eighteen bullets in him—a kind of joint tribute to British courage and American marksmanship! All told, the 14th lost seventeen killed and forty-one wounded. The Virginians had one man slightly wounded.

This bloody little battle has sometimes been called the Bunker Hill of the South. It was strategically useful, for it caused the redcoats to abandon their own earthworks and evacuate Norfolk. In revenge, Dunmore ordered the town flattened, which was done on New Year's Day by the ships' guns. Under cover of the cannonade, a shore party burned the wharves, and the Virginia troops, not to be outdone, burned the rest of the town. It was a loyalist stronghold anyway.

Dunmore then sailed up Chesapeake Bay and tried to establish a base on Gwynn Island. He was driven off—ironically, by Andrew Lewis, now a brigadier general. Unable to find a spot he could hold, Dunmore threw up his hands and sailed for home.

The Declaration of Independence

Virginia was being governed all this while by a series of conventions and committees of public safety, stopgap arrangements to hold things together while men made up their minds: Did they or did they not want to be independent? Finally the opinion began to prevail that Americans had gone too far to back down.

On June 12 the fifth Virginia convention, sitting in Williamsburg,

The resolution presented to the Continental Congress by Richard Henry Lee, calling for independence.

Resolved That these United Colonies are, and of right ought to be, free and independent States, that they are absolved from all allegiance to the British Crown, and that all political connection between them and the State of Great Britain is, and ought to be, totally dissolved.

That it is expedient forthwith to take the most effectual measures for forming foreign Alliances.

That a plan of confederation be prepared and transmitted to the respective Colonies for their consideration and approbation.

unanimously adopted a Declaration of Rights, drawn up by George Mason of Gunston Hall. It set forth the principle that government was responsible to the people and could only govern with their consent, and that when it becomes evil, they have the right to reform it. This Virginia declaration has been called one of the most important documents in the English language. A few weeks later its provisions were included in the Virginia constitution, the first written constitution to be adopted by a modern state.

Meanwhile the determination to declare independence was hardening. On May 15, 1776, Edmund Pendleton introduced a resolution to the convention:

> *Resolved*, That the delegates appointed to represent this colony in General Congress be instructed to propose to that respectable body to declare the United Colonies free and independent states. . . .

Copies were sent immediately to Lee and Wythe in Philadelphia. Peyton Randolph had died the previous fall, but Virginia had an alternate to take his place, and a copy was sent to him, too: Thomas Jefferson.

Richard Henry Lee placed the resolution, worded slightly differently, before the Congress on June 7, and a committee was appointed to draw up a declaration that would explain the reasons the colonists believed they should be independent of Great Britain. The committee left the actual writing to Thomas Jefferson, who was known to have a gift for that sort of thing—a "peculiar felicity of expression," John Adams called it. Accordingly, Jefferson retired to his lodgings at Seventh and High streets and penned the famous document. It was passed by the committee and on to the Congress.

On Monday, July 1, the Congress met, dissolved itself into a committee of the whole, and discussed the wording of the declaration. One clause was struck out—a strongly worded condemnation of slavery, which Jefferson had rather ingeniously blamed on George III. Other minor changes were made. The following day, July 2, a vote was taken, and the measure passed into existence. Jefferson had studded it with phrases of such grace and power that it is still being plagiarized to this day. The key paragraph said:

> We, therefore, the Representatives of the united States of America, in General Congress, Assembled, appealing to the Supreme Judge of the world for the rectitude of our intentions, do, in the Name and by Authority of the good People of these Colonies, solemnly publish and declare, That these United Colonies are, and of Right ought to be Free and Independent States; that they are Absolved from all Allegiance to the British Crown, and that all political connection between them and the State of Great Britain, is and ought to be totally dissolved; and that as Free and Independent States, they have full Power to levy War, conclude Peace, contract Alliances, establish Commerce, and to do all other Acts and Things which Independent States may of right do. And for the support of this Declaration, with a firm reliance on the Protection of Divine Providence, we mutually pledge to each other our Lives, our Fortunes, and our sacred Honor.

On July 4, 1776, it was signed. Signing for Virginia were George Wythe, Richard Henry Lee, Thomas Jefferson, Benjamin Harrison, Thomas Nelson, Jr., Francis Lightfoot Lee, and Carter Braxton.

Virginia Goes to War

Once Dunmore departed, Virginia saw no military action for several years. Yet the state was alive with soldiers. Winchester looked like this to a 1775 visitor:

> Here every Presence is warlike, every sound is martial! Drums beating, Pipes & Bag-Pipes playing, & only sonorous heroic Tunes —Every Man has a hunting-shirt, which is the Uniform of each Company—Almost all have a Cockade, & bucks-tale in their Hats to represent that they are hardy, resolute & invincible Natives of the Woods of America. . . .

One notable Virginia officer was John Peter Gabriel Mühlenberg.

John Peter Gabriel Mühlenberg, minister of the Gospel and brigadier general in the Continental Army.

The son of Henry Melchior Mühlenberg, virtual founder of the Lutheran Church in America, he was educated at Heidelberg for the ministry, but because the Anglican Church was established in Virginia, he had to receive ordination from an English bishop before he could accept an appointment to a German congregation at Woodstock in the Shenandoah Valley. He was serving there, a vigorous supporter of the liberty cause, when the war broke out.

One day, toward the close of 1775, he preached a memorable sermon on a text from Ecclesiastes 3: "To every thing there is a season, and a time to every purpose under the heaven. A time to be born, and a time to die . . . a time to kill and a time to heal; a time to break down and a time to build up . . . a time to love and a time to hate; a time of war and a time of peace. . . ."

Looking out over his congregation, he said, "There is a time to fight, and that time has now come." And, taking off his clerical robe, he revealed under it the uniform of a Virginia colonel. He then turned his sermon into a rousing enlistment speech, ordered the recruiting drums to be beaten at the church door, and talked nearly the entire male membership of his congregation into putting down their names.

Mühlenberg served at Brandywine, Germantown, Valley Forge, Monmouth, Stony Point, and Yorktown. In 1777 he was promoted to brigadier general of Continentals. His men called him Teufel Piet, "Devil Pete," and small wonder.

Congress had voted to organize some rifle companies from among the backwoodsmen of Virginia, Carolina, and Pennsylvania. Most renowned of these was Morgan's Rifles, formed in 1777 by Daniel Morgan, known as the Old Wagoner from his services with the Braddock campaign. Morgan had gone along on the Arnold-Montgomery expedition against Canada in 1775–1776 and had actually penetrated to the heart of Quebec City before he and a small band of followers—unsupported—were surrounded and taken prisoners. The British had been so impressed with this performance that they had offered him a commission as general, and he had turned it down (perhaps because he was still bitter over having been flogged during the Braddock expedition—five hundred lashes for striking an officer). After exchange, Morgan was given command of the 11th Virginia Regiment, which took its more famous name from its colonel.

The Rifles served with deadly effectiveness in the Saratoga campaign. They fanned out through the woods, perched in trees or behind rocks, picked off king's officers almost at will, and were summoned together again by a turkey call. Later they served in the 1779 expedition against the New York Indians and were back in Virginia for the final act there.

Virginians served in innumerable capacities, supplying the Continental Army with regiments of foot, horse, and artillery. In addition, Virginia militia served throughout the rugged Carolina campaigns, and were among the few such units that could be relied on to hold up their end in a formal field of battle. The state made other large contributions to the cause—food for Washington's army and tobacco to uphold the financial credit of the United States abroad. Most dramatic of all, perhaps, was Virginia's service to the frontier.

Kaskaskia and Vincennes

In 1775 Daniel Boone led the first party of settlers through the Cumberland Gap into Kentucky. Throughout the war these settlements were subject to savage raids by Indians, supplied and supported by the British at Fort Detroit. In 1777 a twenty-six-year-old surveyor and militia officer named George Rogers Clark appeared in Williamsburg with a plea that the state take Kentucky under her protection. With the backing of Patrick Henry, now governor, the Assembly voted to create a new county of Kentucky and gave Clark five hundred pounds of gunpowder and its blessing.

Back he went to Kentucky with a daring plan. He recruited a small force–178 men when all the deserters had abandoned the enterprise–and set off by boat down the Ohio. At the falls (modern Louisville) he left the river and traveled overland to the British forts in the Illinois country. There were no king's troops in the vicinity–it had not been thought necessary, four hundred miles from the nearest Americans–and the French militia who were guarding the forts surrendered them without a fight. Kaskaskia and Cahokia on the Mississippi and Vincennes on the Wabash (modern Illinois-Indiana line) fell into the Virginians' hands. It was July, 1778.

On the strength of this victory Virginia created Illinois County and provided the first American administrative structure–albeit only on paper–in the Northwest Territory. Of more immediate importance, this sudden appearance of Americans out of nowhere made a powerful impression on the Indians, who had been led to believe the British were omnipotent.

Detroit heard about these activities, of course, and in December the lieutenant governor of Canada, Major General Henry Hamilton, arrived on the Wabash with six hundred men and retook Vincennes. Five other expeditions were planned for the spring of 1779. They were to invade the Illinois and Ohio countries and expel all American settlers. But they counted without Colonel Clark.

He was on the Mississippi when he heard that the Wabash fort had fallen. He resolved to retake it at once. He had fewer than 90 men, because most of his original force had returned to Kentucky, but by inducing some of the French to enlist, he swelled this total to 170. On February 5, 1779, they set off on what was to be an epic journey.

The winter had been mild and rainy. In the flat prairies of southern Illinois, every stream had turned into a lake. The column waded nearly the whole of their 150-mile advance, often waist deep. At night they built scaffolds to hold their powder and provisions and slept themselves in the mud. A chill rain fell most of the time, and they were short of food. Once across the Wabash, they found themselves with seven miles still to traverse—and the flood so deep that it was over some men's heads. Nevertheless they pushed on, the shorter men clinging to a makeshift canoe which towed them across the deeper patches.

On February 23, they came within sight of the town. Disguising the smallness of his numbers, Clark sent advance warning to the townspeople to stay out of sight, and when he arrived at nightfall, not a soul was to be seen. The inhabitants of Vincennes were nearly all French, and they had not bothered to warn the fort that Americans were nearby. They even fed Clark's starving men.

He surrounded the fort with his little army and opened an all-night barrage. The British were stupefied at his popping up out of nowhere in this fashion, especially since they did not know how small the American force was. The fort was armed with cannon, but Clark's riflemen were so deft at firing through the opened gunports that the guns could scarcely be used. They also picked off the defending garrison by poking rifle barrels between the pickets of the stockade. After a night and part of a day of this demoralizing siege, Hamilton surrendered.

Because he was the commander at Fort Detroit, which was the source for the supplies that kept the war parties going, Hamilton was the most hated man on the frontier, nicknamed the Hair Buyer General. Clark sent him to Williamsburg a prisoner, and he was kept in the public jail more than a year—the only prisoner of war Americans refused to parole.

Clark's ultimate dream—using Vincennes as a base from which to

Thomas Jefferson, as governor of the new state, pursuaded the Burgesses to move the capital to Richmond.

take Detroit—never materialized. But when word of Hamilton's surrender reached the other British expeditions against the frontier, it stopped all five of them dead in their tracks.

The South Invaded

In May, 1779, Virginia was invaded briefly by a British naval force, which captured Portsmouth. Using that town as a base, the British sent out raiding parties, destroyed thousands of barrels of provisions and other supplies, and seized several thousand hogsheads of tobacco. After they burned Suffolk, they departed without losing a man.

A month later Thomas Jefferson replaced Patrick Henry as governor. The ease with which the British could control the rivers made Williamsburg too exposed a site for Virginia's government. Jefferson persuaded the burgesses to move the capital to Richmond—then a little one-street village of eighteen hundred inhabitants—and this was carried out in the spring of 1780. As it turned out, Richmond's site wasn't much safer than Williamsburg's.

Jefferson had become governor at a disastrous moment, for the British were just then turning their attention to the South. In May, 1780, they captured Charleston, South Carolina, and under command of Major General Charles Earl Cornwallis, marched into the interior of the Carolinas, occupying forts and trying to rouse Loyalist support. Jefferson sent Virginia militia to the aid of American forces under Horatio Gates, but in August Gates bungled it all away at the rout of Camden, and the South lay prostrate.

Somehow another army was scraped together and Nathanael Greene appointed to command it, and the tide began to turn. Greene had learned all his tactics out of books, but he had learned them well, and he had his professional opponent outclassed from the start. Greene fought three battles, lost them all, ran the king's troops all over the countryside, and won his campaign.

Meanwhile, Virginia was in trouble from other sources. In December, 1780, Benedict Arnold, who had deserted to the king's side the previous October, landed at Westover with a detachment of British troops and marched on the new capital.

Virginia had strained her own resources to help other states. Over two thousand Virginians had been captured by the British at Charleston alone. The treasury was empty, and the state had exhausted itself supplying food and arms. The militiamen that Jefferson managed to raise and send to bar Arnold's path were bottom-of-the-barrel material. They fled from their position without firing a shot. On January 5, 1781, Arnold entered Richmond.

He stayed only long enough to burn some buildings and send out a party to destroy stores of gunpowder and ironworks. He had hoped to capture Jefferson as well, but the governor had escaped to the protection of Baron von Steuben, commanding a small detachment of Continentals a few miles away. Steuben marched against Arnold, but the king's forces brushed him aside and returned safely to Portsmouth, where they spent the winter. They were reinforced there in the spring of 1781.

Virginia was nearly helpless. The British army could roam about the state at will. Washington—himself stuck outside New York, where he was keeping an eye on the main body of king's troops under Clinton—sent Lafayette with three regiments of light infantry to do what he could. The marquis's arrival caused the British, who had raided as far up the Appomattox as Petersburg, to pull back but not to retreat very far.

Cornwallis in Virginia

At this juncture Lord Cornwallis got tired of dodging and weaving with Greene in the Carolinas and crossed the Dan into Virginia. He joined forces with Arnold at Petersburg and started after Lafayette, who retreated before him. ("I am not strong enough even to get beaten," Lafayette reported ruefully of his command.) Cornwallis was nervous about getting too far from the rivers, where he could count on British naval support, so he camped on a tributary of the Pamunkey, some miles above Richmond. From there he sent his cavalry commander, Lieutenant Colonel Banastre Tarleton, to seize Jefferson and the rest of the government, now refugeeing in Charlottesville.

The horsemen rode off but stopped along the way at the Cuckoo Tavern in Louisa County. Captain John Jouett of the militia saw them, guessed their mission, slipped out ahead of them, and rode through the woods and fields to warn the government. Battered and scratched by low-hanging branches, Jouett traveled all night and arrived ahead of the troopers. (In Jefferson's case, only just ahead, for he left Monticello, his estate just outside Charlottesville, a bare ten minutes before the first soldiers rode in.) For endurance and stamina, Jouett's horse deserves as much praise as its master—Jouett was six feet four and weighed over two hundred pounds.

Tarleton did manage to seize some members of the government, however, and destroyed many public records. He also liberated about twenty British prisoners of war who had been interned in the Charlottesville area.

When the cavalry had rejoined him, Cornwallis decided to move

Major General Charles Earl Cornwallis, commander of the royal forces in Virginia.

eastward and establish his headquarters at some seaport. With Lafayette nipping at his heels, he marched down the peninsula, first settled at Portsmouth, then changed his mind and moved across the James to Yorktown. On August 22, 1781, he began to fortify the place. Lafayette, Steuben, and Anthony Wayne camped nearby with orders not to let him get away.

On August 27, Washington and Rochambeau broke their northern camps and headed south.

Yorktown

Americans had signed a treaty of alliance with the French in the winter of 1778, but so far had had little military benefit from it. Now word had come that Admiral Comte de Grasse was sailing from the West Indies for Chesapeake Bay with twenty-nine ships and three thousand men. If the French fleet could cut off Cornwallis' escape by sea and a joint French-American army surround him by land, he might be forced to surrender. Accordingly, the French squadron at Newport

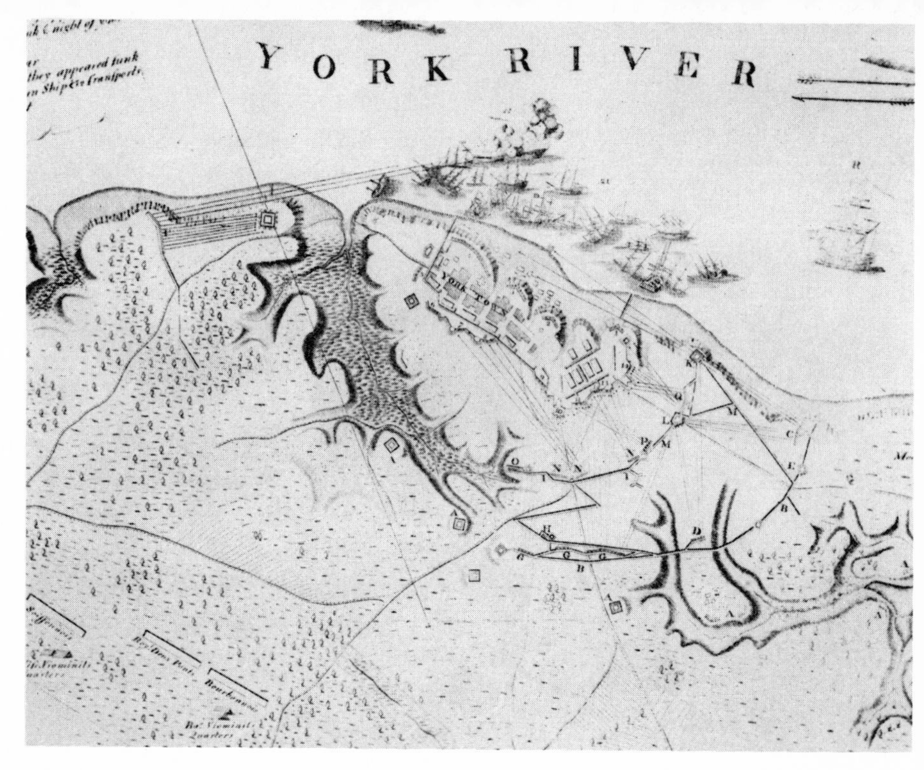

Yorktown under siege by French and American troops. Swamps protected her on the west, so attacks concentrated on the eastern flank.

loaded up the siege artillery and sailed for Yorktown, and the foot soldiers of the two armies hotfooted to join them.

A British fleet under Admiral Thomas Graves had sailed from New York to catch the Newport squadron, but when it peeked into York River, it found de Grasse's big West Indies fleet instead. The two naval forces sailed out on September 5 to do battle.

It was an indecisive conflict. The two forces blazed away at each other most of the first afternoon, then were separated off and on by storms for four days. When the weather cleared on September 9, the British discovered that the Newport squadron had arrived, and since de Grasse's fleet alone outnumbered them, this reinforcement made the odds too long. Graves sailed back to New York and left Cornwallis to his fate.

The land troops began to straggle into Williamsburg, thirteen miles from Yorktown, on September 14. By the twenty-fifth, the last of them had arrived, and on the thirtieth the outworks of Yorktown, which the British had abandoned as untenable, were occupied. As the big guns arrived, siege operations were begun, and the first trench was opened on October 5. Four days later the flags were run up and the first guns opened on the British lines.

Wrote James Thacher, an American army surgeon, of this bombardment:

> From the 10th to the 15th, a tremendous and incessant firing from the American and French batteries is kept up, and the enemy return the fire, but with little effect. . . . The bombshells from the besiegers and the besieged are incessantly crossing each other's path in the air. They are clearly visible in the form of a black ball in the day, but in the night they appear like a fiery meteor with a blazing tail. . . .

Lord Cornwallis was soon viewing his situation as desperate. He wrote to Sir Henry Clinton, his superior, in New York: "If you cannot relieve me very soon, you must be prepared to hear the worst." The little town was raked by cannon fire; eighty civilians were killed, houses flattened. British defenses were so torn up that they could scarcely reply to this barrage. Still they hung on doggedly.

On the eleventh, the second parallel trench was opened. Two British redoubts, called Number Nine and Number Ten, overlooked this trench and had to be stormed. On the night of the fourteenth, therefore, the double assault was launched—the French on Number Nine, the Americans on Number Ten. A Yankee sergeant thus described his share in this attack:

> The enemy discovered us and directly opened a sharp fire upon us. We were now at a place where many of our large shells had burst in the ground, making holes sufficient to bury an ox in. The men, having their eyes fixed upon what was transacting be-

Cornwallis surrenders the troops under his command to Washington and Rochambeau, October 19, 1781.

> fore them, were every now and then falling into these holes. I thought the British were killing us off at a great rate. At length, one of the holes happening to pick me up, I found out the mystery of the huge slaughter.

By morning the redoubts were part of the finished second parallel, and the earl was in big trouble. He decided on a desperate course. He had seized and fortified Gloucester Point on the other side of the river when he first reached the area. Now he notified Tarleton, in command at Gloucester, that he was going to try to cross the York and break out of the encirclement. The attempt was made the night of the sixteenth, but before more than a few boatloads of men had crossed over, a storm came up and drove them back.

The following day, about ten o'clock, a king's officer was seen to mount the Yorktown parapet, waving a white handkerchief. There was a drummer boy with him, and as the guns slowly fell silent, the allies could hear what call he was beating: the parley.

Lord Cornwallis proposed that a twenty-four-hour truce be agreed upon "to settle terms for the surrender of the post of York and Gloucester." Washington agreed, wrote his stipulations, and sent two officers to treat with Cornwallis' representatives. It took until the following day before the terms were hammered out. While they waited, the opposing armies stood on their respective parapets and stared at one another across the no-man's-land. Then on October 19, 1781, the formal surrender ceremony was enacted in a field in front of the town.

A Virginia soldier described the scene:

> The British troops marched out of Yorktown in solid columns, between the lines of the American army into an old field, where they deposited first their drums with the fifes on the heads of the drums, struck their colors into the soil, laid their guns on the ground, faced about and marched back into Yorktown.

It is believed that the tune the fifers played as they marched out

A contemporary watercolor sketch of Yorktown, the sleepy tobacco port that saw the end of the Revolution.

of their fortifications was a ballad called "The World Turned Upside Down."

The Commonwealth of Virginia

The decisive victory at Yorktown ended active fighting. The British still held New York City and Charleston, but they were now deeply committed to fighting France's European allies, Spain and Holland, and had no energy to spare for another American campaign. Or much heart. In 1782 Great Britain recognized the independence of the thirteen American states, and the following year the war was ended by the Treaty of Paris. So the little tobacco port on the York was the true scene of British withdrawal from control of the United States.

Jamestown and Yorktown are twenty miles apart. It took Virginians 174 years to travel from one to the other and in the course of that journey to change from Englishmen to Virginians to Americans. Citizens of the Commonwealth of Virginia would remember their childhood as "his Majesty's most ancient and loyal colony" with fondness: Patrick Henry orating in the House . . . the Publick Times . . . Young Buckskins at the side of his ill-fated general . . . Spotswood and his friends on their journey through the mountains . . . the tobacco fleet in Chesapeake Bay . . . the old governor and the young rebel . . . Opechancanough plotting desperate measures . . . Pocahontas and her father's captive . . . the three small ships amoor in the river beside the brand-new settlement. . . .

But childhood was over now, and by and large Virginians were glad to be adults. There was a great deal to be done.

Bibliography

American Heritage, *History of the Thirteen Colonies*. New York, American Heritage Publishing Company, 1967.

Andrews, Charles M., ed., *Narratives of the Insurrections, 1675–1690*. New York, Barnes & Noble, Inc., 1952.

Andrews, Matthew Page, *Virginia, the Old Dominion*. Garden City, N.Y., Doubleday & Company, Inc., 1937.

Barbour, Philip L., *The Jamestown Voyages Under the First Charter, 1606–1609*, 2 vols. New York, Cambridge University Press, 1969.

——— *Pocahontas and Her World*. Boston, Houghton Mifflin Company, 1969.

Bemis, Samuel M., ed., *The Three Charters of the Virginia Company of London*. Williamsburg, Va., 350th Anniversary Celebration Corporation, 1957.

Beverley, Robert, *The History and Present State of Virginia*, Louis B. Wright, ed. Charlottesville, Va., University Press of Virginia, 1969.

Billings, E. R., *Tobacco: Its History, Varieties, Culture, Manufactures, and Commerce*. Hartford, Conn., American Publishing Company, 1875.

Boucher, John Newton, *A Century and a Half of Pittsburg*. Pittsburgh, Lewis Publishing Company, 1908.

Bowen, Catherine Drinker, *John Adams and the American Revolution*. Boston, Atlantic Monthly Press, 1950.

Brooks, Jerome E., *The Mighty Leaf: Tobacco Through the Ages*. Boston, Little, Brown and Company, 1952.

Brown, Alexander, *The First Republic in America*. Boston, Houghton Mifflin Company, 1898.

Castiglione, Arturo, "Tobacco," *CIBA Symposium*, February–March, 1943.

Chamberlain, Samuel, *Behold Williamsburg*. New York, Hastings House, 1947.

Chitwood, Oliver P., *A History of Colonial America*. New York, Harper and Row, 1961.

Commager, Henry Steele, ed., *Documents of American History*. New York, Appleton-Century-Crofts, 1963.

———, and Morris, Richard B., eds., *The Spirit of 'Seventy-Six*, 2 vols. New York, Bobbs-Merrill Company, Inc., 1958.

Craig, Neville B., *Washington's First Campaign*. Pittsburgh, Wright & Charlton, 1848.

Craven, Wesley Frank, *The Colonies in Transition*. New York, Harper and Row, 1968.

———, *The Southern Colonies in the Seventeenth Century, 1607–1689.* Baton Rouge, La., Louisiana State University Press, 1949.
Davis, Burke, *A Williamsburg Galaxy.* New York, Holt, Rinehart and Winston, 1968.
Davis, Richard Beale, ed., *William Fitzhugh and His Chesapeake World.* Chapel Hill, N.C., University of North Carolina Press, 1963.
Dickerson, Oliver M., *The Navigation Acts and the American Revolution.* Philadelphia, University of Pennsylvania Press, 1951.
Earle, Alice Morse, *Home Life in Colonial Days.* New York, The Macmillan Company, 1898.
Fairholt, F. W., *Tobacco: Its History and Associations.* London, Chapman and Hall, 1859.
Farish, Hunter Dickinson, ed., *The Journal and Letters of Philip Vickers Fithian.* Williamsburg, Va., Colonial Williamsburg, Inc., 1957.
Farrar, Emmie F., *Old Virginia Houses.* New York, Hastings House, 1955.
Fishwick, Marshall W., *Virginia: A New Look at the Old Dominion.* New York, Harper and Row, 1959.
Forman, Henry Chandlee, *Virginia Architecture in the Seventeenth Century.* Williamsburg, Va., 350th Anniversary Celebration Corporation, 1957.
Freeman, Douglas S., *George Washington: A Biography,* 7 vols. New York, Charles Scribner's Sons, 1948–1957.
Gutman, Judith M., *The Colonial Venture.* New York, Basic Books, 1966.
Hamilton, Charles, ed., *Braddock's Defeat.* Norman, Okla., University of Oklahoma Press, 1959.
Hatch, Charles E., Jr., *Jamestown, Virginia.* Historical Handbook Series, No. 2. Washington, D.C., Government Printing Office, 1952.
Hume, Ivor Noel, *Here Lies Virginia.* New York, Alfred A. Knopf, Inc., 1963.
——— *1775: Another Part of the Field.* New York, Alfred A. Knopf, Inc., 1966.
Jefferson, Thomas, *Papers of Thomas Jefferson,* Julian P. Boyd, ed., 17 vols. Princeton, N.J., Princeton University Press, 1950–.
Jones, Hugh, *The Present State of Virginia,* Richard L. Morton, ed. Chapel Hill, N.C., University of North Carolina Press, 1956.
Kingsbury, Susan M., *Records of the Virginia Company of London,* 4 vols. Washington, D.C., Government Printing Office, 1906–1935.
Langdon, William Chauncy, *Everyday Things in American Life, 1607–1776.* New York, Charles Scribner's Sons, 1937.
Lossing, B. J., *Pictorial Field-Book of the Revolution.* New York, Harper Brothers, 1850.
Martin, Joseph Plumb, *Private Yankee Doodle,* George F. Scheer, ed. Boston, Little, Brown and Company, 1962.
Mason, Frances N., ed., *John Norton & Sons: Merchants of London and Virginia.* Richmond, Va., Dietz Press, Inc., 1937.

Mathison, Richard, *The Eternal Search*. New York, G. P. Putnam's Sons, 1958.

McIlwaine, H. R., et al., eds, *Executive Journals of the Council of Colonial Virginia*, 6 vols. Richmond, Va., The Colonial Press, 1925–1966.

McIlwaine, H. R., and Kennedy, J. P., eds., *Journals of the House of Burgesses of Virginia, 1619–1776*, 13 vols. Richmond, Va., The Colonial Press, 1905–1915.

Morgan, Edmund S., *Virginians at Home: Family Life in the Eighteenth Century*. Charlottesville, Va., University Press of Virginia, 1963.

——— and Helen M., *The Stamp Act Crisis*. New York, Collier Books, 1963.

Morison, Samuel Eliot, ed., *Sources and Documents Illustrating the American Revolution, 1764–1788*. New York, Clarendon Press, 1929.

Morton, Richard L., *Colonial Virginia*, 2 vols. Chapel Hill, N.C., University of North Carolina Press, 1960.

Mulkearn, Lois, and Pugh, Edwin V., *Traveler's Guide to Historic Western Pennsylvania*. Pittsburgh, University of Pittsburgh Press, 1953.

National Geographic Society, *America's Historylands*. Washington, D.C., The National Geographic Society, 1962.

——— *The Revolutionary War*. Washington, D.C., The National Geographic Society, 1967.

——— *This England*. Washington, D.C., The National Geographic Society, 1966.

Niles, Blair, *The James*. Rivers of America Series. New York, Farrar and Rinehart, 1939.

Peckham, Howard H., *The Colonial Wars, 1689–1762*. Chicago, University of Chicago Press, 1964.

Pomfret, John E., and Shumway, Floyd M., *Founding the American Colonies, 1583–1660*. New American Nation Series. New York, Harper and Row, 1970.

Proceedings of the Convention of Delegates held at the Capitol . . . 6 May 1776. Richmond, Va., 1816, Early American Imprints, American Antiquarian Society.

Quarles, Benjamin, *The Negro in the Making of America*. New York, Collier Books, 1964.

Rankin, Hugh F., *The Golden Age of Piracy*. Williamsburg, Va., Colonial Williamsburg, Inc., 1969.

Redman, Alvin, *The House of Hanover*. New York, Funk and Wagnalls, 1968.

Scheer, George F., and Rankin, Hugh F., *Rebels and Redcoats*. New York, New American Library, 1957.

Smith, Bradford, *Captain John Smith: His Life and Legend*. Philadelphia, J. B. Lippincott Company, 1953.

Smith, John, *Travels and Works of Captain John Smith*, Edward Arber, ed. Edinburgh, J. Grant, 1910.

Tingling, Marion, and Davies, Godfrey, eds., *The Western Country in 1793: Reports on Kentucky and Virginia by Harry Toulmun*. San Marino, Calif., Huntington Library and Art Gallery, 1948.
Tyler, Lyon G., ed., *Narratives of Early Virginia, 1606–1625*. New York, Charles Scribner's Sons, 1907.
Van Every, Dale, *A Company of Heroes, The American Frontier, 1775–1783*. New York, William Morrow and Company, Inc., 1962.
Van Schreeven, William J., and Reese, George H., eds., *Proceedings of the General Assembly of Virginia*, Jamestown, Va., 1969.
Virginia Gazette, 1736–1780.
Virginia Magazine of History and Biography, Volumes 1, 5, 7, 8, 24, and 30.
Washburn, Wilcomb E., *The Governor and the Rebel*. Chapel Hill, N.C., University of North Carolina Press, 1957.
Washington, George, *The Journal of Major George Washington*, facsimile edition. Ann Arbor, Mich., University of Michigan Microfilm, 1966.
Wertenbaker, Thomas J., *The Middle Colonies, The Founding of American Civilization*. New York, Cooper Square Publishers, 1963.
——— *Patrician and Plebeian in Virginia*. New York, Russell and Russell, 1959.
——— *The Planters of Colonial Virginia*. New York, Russell and Russell, 1959.
——— *Torchbearer of the Revolution, The Story of Bacon's Rebellion and its Leader*. Gloucester, Mass., Peter Smith, Publisher, 1940.
——— *Virginia Under the Stuarts, 1607–1688*. New York, Russell and Russell, 1959.
William and Mary Quarterly, 1st series, vol. 9, 2d series, vol. 10.
Williams, Neville, *Contraband Cargoes: Seven Centuries of Smuggling*. London, Longmans, Green and Co., Ltd., 1959.
Willison, George F., *Behold Virginia! The Fifth Crown*. New York, Harcourt, Brace and Company, 1951.
Wirt, William, *Sketches of the Life and Character of Patrick Henry*. Philadelphia, James Webster, 1818.
Woodward, Marcus, ed., *Leaves from Gerard's Herball*. New York, Dover Publishing Company, 1969.
Wright, Louis B., *The Cultural Life of the American Colonies*. New American Nation Series. New York, Harper and Brothers, 1957.
——— *The First Gentlemen of Virginia*. Charlottesville, Va., University Press of Virginia, 1964.

Important Dates

April 19, 1585	The first English expedition to colonize America sets out from Plymouth.
August 1587	Settlement established at Roanoke Island—the "Lost Colony."
December 20, 1606	The *Susan Constant*, the *Godspeed*, and the *Discovery* leave England for Virginia under command of Captain Christopher Newport.
April 26, 1607	Newport's three ships arrive in Chesapeake Bay.
May 13, 1607	Newport's ships arrive at Jamestown Island.
May 23, 1609	The king issues a new charter to the Virginia Company.
June 28, 1613	John Rolfe's first crop of West Indian tobacco is shipped to England.
April 1614	John Rolfe and Pocahontas are married at Jamestown.
1617	Pocahontas dies in England.
July 30, 1619	The General Assembly of the Colony of Virginia, America's first representative assembly, meets at Jamestown.
November 17, 1619	The first Negro servants are brought to Virginia.
March 22, 1622	Indians attack English settlers all over the colony and kill about one third of them.
May 24, 1624	The Virginia Company is dissolved and Virginia becomes a royal colony.
1634	Virginia is divided into counties—the foundation of local government.
February 1641	Sir William Berkeley is appointed governor of Virginia; arrives to take office 1642.
April 18, 1644	Indians attack settlers, killing about five hundred.
January 30, 1649	Parliamentary rule begins in England with the execution of Charles I.
March 12, 1652	Virginia surrenders to parliamentary forces.
March 21, 1660	Berkeley reinstalled as governor.
May 29, 1660	Charles II returns to English throne.
April 1676	Nathaniel Bacon is selected by the frontiersmen to lead a campaign against the Indians.

June 9, 1676	Bacon is captured and pardoned by the Governor.
August 1676	Governor Berkeley flees to Eastern Shore in the face of open rebellion.
September 19, 1676	Bacon burns Jamestown.
October 1676	Bacon dies in Gloucester and the rebellion collapses.
May 5, 1677	Governor Berkeley returns to England.
1680	Lord Culpeper arrives as governor and soon departs.
1685	Charles II dies and is succeeded by his Roman Catholic brother, James II.
1688	William and Mary ascend the British throne and sign the Declaration of Rights.
June 3, 1690	Francis Nicholson becomes Governor of Virginia.
February 8, 1693	King William and Queen Mary issue a charter for the College of William and Mary in Virginia.
October 27, 1699	Capital of Virginia is moved to Middle Plantation, renamed Williamsburg.
1705	Robert Beverley's *History and Present State of Virginia* is published in England.
June 23, 1710	A new governor, Alexander Spotswood, arrives in Virginia.
August 20, 1716	Governor Spotswood sets out from Williamsburg with his "Knights of the Golden Horseshoe" on a trip over the Blue Ridge Mountains.
November 1718	The pirate Blackbeard is killed by an expedition from Virginia.
1724	*The Present State of Virginia* by Hugh Jones is published in England.
February 22, 1732	George Washington born in Westmoreland County.
August 6, 1736	The first issue of the *Virginia Gazette* is published in Williamsburg.
April 13, 1743	Thomas Jefferson is born in Albemarle County.
January 16, 1754	Washington returns from the Ohio Valley with a report that the French intend to take over the region.
May 28, 1754	Washington's troops exchange shots with a French force and the French and Indian War begins.

July 4, 1754	Washington surrenders Fort Necessity to the French.
July 9, 1755	General Edward Braddock's army is defeated by the French and their Indian allies near Fort Duquesne.
August 14, 1755	Governor Dinwiddie makes George Washington commander-in-chief of all Virginia forces.
November 25, 1758	Fort Duquesne is captured by the British.
May 30, 1765	Patrick Henry makes his famous "treason" speech against the Stamp Act.
November 1, 1765	The Stamp Act goes into effect.
1766	Richard Bland publishes his *An Inquiry into the Rights of the British Colonies.*
March 18, 1766	The Stamp Act is repealed.
September 1771	Lord Dunmore, Virginia's last royal Governor, arrives in the colony.
January 1774	Virginia seizes Pittsburgh.
May 27, 1774	Virginia proposes a Continental Congress.
October 1774	Lord Dunmore marches against Ohio Valley Indians.
October 10, 1774	Battle of Point Pleasant; Shawnees under Cornstalk are defeated by Virginians under Andrew Lewis.
March 23, 1775	Patrick Henry delivers his "Liberty or Death" speech at the second Virginia Convention in Richmond.
April 20, 1775	Dunmore removes powder from the Williamsburg magazine.
June 8, 1775	Dunmore announces that he considers Williamsburg no longer safe for him and moves to British warship.
December 9, 1775	Colonial troops defeat Dunmore's force at Great Bridge.
May 15, 1776	The Virginia Convention adopts a resolution introduced by Edmund Pendleton, instructing the delegates to the Continental Congress to urge Congress "to declare the United Colonies free and independent States."
June 28, 1776	The Convention adopts a new constitution for the state.

June 29, 1776	Patrick Henry is chosen the first Governor of the Commonwealth of Virginia.
July 1776	Dunmore is driven from Virginia.
July 4, 1776	Declaration of Independence is signed in Philadelphia.
July 4, 1778	George Rogers Clark captures Kaskaskia.
February 25, 1779	Clark recaptures Vincennes and secures the Northwest Territory from British control.
May 1779	The British first capture Portsmouth.
June 1, 1779	Thomas Jefferson is elected governor.
August 31, 1779	Agreement is reached between representatives of Virginia and representatives of Pennsylvania, establishing the western boundary of the latter.
April 1780	The capital is moved from Williamsburg to Richmond.
October 19, 1781	Cornwallis surrenders his army to the Americans and French at Yorktown.
1784	Virginia gives up her claims to territory north of the Ohio.
June 25, 1788	Virginia ratifies the United States Constitution.

Historic Sites

Augusta Stone Presbyterian Church, Augusta County, was built between 1747 and 1749 and is the oldest surviving church in the Shenandoah Valley.

Bacon's Castle, Surry County, was built by Arthur Allen about 1655. It is one of the oldest houses in Virginia. It was seized by the followers of Nathaniel Bacon in 1676. It is privately owned.

Berkeley, Charles City County, was built in 1726 by Benjamin Harrison IV. It was the birthplace of Benjamin Harrison V, signer of the Declaration of Independence and Governor of Virginia, and of William Henry Harrison, ninth President of the United States. It is privately owned but open to the public.

Cape Henry Memorial. A granite cross marks the point where the Jamestown settlers made their first landing on Virginia soil. The site is within the Fort Story military reservation in the City of Virginia Beach. It is maintained by the National Park Service.

Capitol of Virginia. The central part of the building was designed by Thomas Jefferson and completed in 1792. The Capitol, in the City of Richmond, is the meeting place of the oldest legislative assembly in the Western Hemisphere.

Carter's Grove, James City County, was built in 1751 by Carter Burwell. The house is maintained by the Colonial Williamsburg Foundation.

College of William and Mary, Williamsburg, is the second-oldest college in the United States. It was chartered by King William and Queen Mary in 1693. The Wren Building, completed in 1697, is the oldest academic building in America. The Phi Beta Kappa Society was founded here in 1776.

Cumberland Gap National Historical Park. The pass in the Cumberland Mountains through which thousands of pioneers traveled during the eighteenth century on their way to Kentucky and the West. The park is maintained by the National Park Service.

Gadsby's Tavern. This tavern was built in Alexandria in 1752. George Washington was a frequent visitor, and Lafayette was entertained here in 1824.

George Washington Birthplace National Monument, near Fredericksburg, includes most of the plantation where Washington was born. There is a gristmill built about 1713 near the house. It is maintained by the National Park Service.

Gunston Hall, Fairfax County, was the home of George Mason, author of the Virginia Bill of Rights. The house, built in 1758, is owned by the Commonwealth of Virginia and administered by the National Society of the Colonial Dames of America.

Jamestown. The site of the first permanent English settlement in North America. It was the capital of Virginia from 1607 to 1699. The site, which includes excavated foundations of several seventeenth-century buildings, is maintained by the National Park Service and the Association for the Preservation of Virginia Antiquities.

Kenmore, Fredericksburg, was the home of George Washington's sister Betty and her husband, Fielding Lewis. It was built about 1752 and is maintained by the Kenmore Association.

Mariners' Museum, Newport News, contains a large collection of ship models, navigational instruments, and a fine research library.

Mary Washington House, Fredericksburg, was purchased in 1772 by George Washington for his mother, who lived there until her death in 1789. It is maintained by the Association for the Preservation of Virginia Antiquities.

Monticello, Albemarle County, was the home of Thomas Jefferson, who designed it and began its construction in 1770. Jefferson and members of his family are buried in a nearby graveyard. The building is maintained by the Thomas Jefferson Memorial Foundation.

Montpelier, Orange County, was the home of James Madison, fourth President of the United States.The house was built about 1760 by Madison's father, and Madison himself later made additions to it. It is privately owned.

Mount Vernon, Fairfax County, was the home of George Washington, who inherited it from his half brother, Lawrence Washington. The house was completed in its present form by 1787. Washington and his wife are buried in a tomb near the house. The plantation is maintained by the Mount Vernon Ladies' Association.

Natural Bridge, Rockbridge County, was described by Thomas Jefferson as "the most sublime of Nature's works."

Scotchtown, Hanover County, was built about 1719 and was the home of Patrick Henry from 1771 to 1778. The house is maintained by the Association for the Preservation of Virginia Antiquities.

Shadwell, Albemarle County, was the birthplace of Thomas Jefferson. The original house was built about 1737 and destroyed by fire in 1770. A reconstruction stands on the original foundations. It is maintained by the Thomas Jefferson Birthplace Memorial Park Commission.

Shirley, Charles City County, was built about 1769 by Charles Carter. The land of this James River Plantation was patented in 1660 by the builder's great-grandfather. It is privately owned but is open to the public.

St. John's Church, Richmond. In this church, built in 1741, Patrick Henry made his famous "Liberty or Death" speech in 1775.

St. Luke's Church, Isle of Wight County, was probably built in 1682. Some people assign 1632 as the date of its construction. It is restored to its original appearance.

Stratford Hall, Westmoreland County, was built by Thomas Lee about 1730. It was the birthplace of Richard Henry Lee and his brother, Francis Lightfoot Lee, signers of the Declaration of Independence. The plantation is maintained by the Robert E. Lee Memorial Foundation.

Thoroughgood House, City of Virginia Beach, was built between 1636 and 1640 by Adam Thoroughgood, and is one of the oldest buildings in North America. It is maintained by the City of Norfolk.

Tuckahoe, Goochland County, was built about 1712 by Thomas Randolph. Thomas Jefferson lived here as a boy. The house is privately owned.

Westover, Charles City County, was the home of the Byrd family and was built about 1730. The house is privately owned.

Williamsburg. The capital of Virginia from 1699 to 1780, it has been restored to its eighteenth-century appearance. Among the restored or reconstructed buildings are the Capitol, the Governor's Palace, the Wren Building of the College of William and Mary, Bruton Parish Church, the Raleigh Tavern, and many homes and shops.

Yorktown. The scene of the final major battle of the Revolutionary War. The battlefield and the Moore House, where the surrender was negotiated, are maintained by the National Park Service.

Index